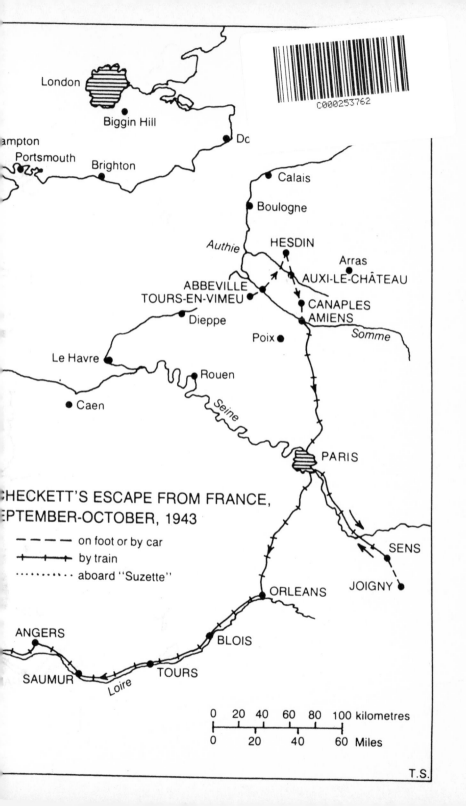

London

Biggin Hill

ampton
Portsmouth    Brighton

Dc

Calais

Boulogne

*Authie*    HESDIN

Arras

AUXI-LE-CHÂTEAU

ABBEVILLE
TOURS-EN-VIMEU    CANAPLES
AMIENS

Dieppe

Poix    *Somme*

Le Havre

Rouen

Caen    *Seine*

PARIS

CHECKETT'S ESCAPE FROM FRANCE,
SEPTEMBER–OCTOBER, 1943

— — — —  on foot or by car
———+——+——  by train
· · · · · · · · · ·  aboard "Suzette"

SENS

JOIGNY

ORLEANS

ANGERS

BLOIS

SAUMUR    TOURS
*Loire*

| 0 | 20 | 40 | 60 | 80 | 100 kilometres |
| 0 | | 20 | 40 | | 60 Miles |

T.S.

# Johnny Checketts:
# THE ROAD
# TO BIGGIN HILL

A Gripping Story of Courage in the Air
and Evasion on the Ground

*Vincent Orange*

Grub Street • London

IN MEMORY
OF THOSE FRENCHMEN AND FRENCHWOMEN
WHO RISKED THEIR LIVES IN
SEPTEMBER AND OCTOBER 1943
SO THAT JOHNNY CHECKETTS MIGHT EVADE
CAPTURE AND RETURN TO ACTIVE SERVICE
AGAINST NAZI GERMANY

First published in 1986

This amended and updated edition published in 2006 by
Grub Street Publishing, 4 Rainham Close, London SW11 6SS

© Grub Street Publishing
© Text Vincent Orange

**A CIP catalogue record for this book
is available from the British Library**

**ISBN-10: 1-904943-79-9**

Printed and bound by MPG Ltd, Bodmin, Cornwall

Distributed in New Zealand by Forrester Books,
19 Tarndale Grove, Albany, Auckland, New Zealand.

# Contents

# Acknowledgements

I know that Johnny and Natalie Checketts would join me in thanking John Davies of Grub Street, London, for agreeing to reprint this biography with a new top and tail, plus some additional photographs. Luke Norsworthy (of Grub Street) and Matthew O'Sullivan (Keeper of Photographs at the RNZAF Museum, Wigram) have given essential support. I remain grateful to Alan Deere and David Crooks for their contributions; also to Ann Tindley, Errol Martyn, David McIntyre, David Gunby and Christina Goulter who read early drafts and made helpful comments. More than ninety men and women wrote to me or telephoned in answer to letters in the press requesting information about Johnny. They will, I hope, understand that I could not find space for everything they told me, nor can they all be named here.

But I must renew special thanks to Mme Massé Solange, M René Guitard, Nicole Verrier, Edith Kearins and her son Rory; to Henry Probert (Air Historical Branch), Fred Lake (Adastral Library), both Ministry of Defence, London, and Ray Grover, National Archives, Wellington. Members of the Ferguson family in Surrey (Bob and Vera, Dennis and Phyllis, Derek and Marion) made young Johnny live for me. At Wigram, Ross Donaldson, John Barry and Nancy Dunn kept an older Johnny alive. Not least do I thank Doug Brown for his invaluable letters. Tony Shatford (Geography Department, University of Canterbury) translated my rough sketches into excellent maps and the ever-obliging staff of the university's Photographic Department were a pleasure to deal with. I remain grateful to the University of Canterbury for research grants and study leave. My wife Sandra not only insulates me from most of life's ordinary hassles but also solves the electronic ones as well. Finally, many thanks to all members of the Checketts family, past and present, who made my trek along the road to Biggin Hill such a pleasant one.

# Foreword

It gives me great pleasure to write this foreword to Vincent Orange's biography of Johnny Checketts, a colleague of mine in war and a firm friend then and now.

As the title implies, the story revolves mostly around the Royal Air Force station at Biggin Hill where, first as a flight commander and later in command of a squadron, Johnny achieved prominence as a fighter pilot. As wing leader there at the time, I can vouch for the accuracy with which the author has captured the day-to-day tension of operations and the personal ups and downs of a fighter pilot's lot during those hectic days.

It was during this period of his operational career that Johnny Checketts was shot down for the second time. On the first occasion he was rescued from his dinghy after having baled out over the English Channel. The second time he was not so lucky, his parachute descent landing him in enemy country in France. The account of his eventual escape, after many weeks in hiding, makes for absorbing reading. In survival and escape, Johnny displayed a singleness of purpose which characterised his approach to air operations, an attribute which enabled him to outpace, after a slow start, most of his contemporaries in the field of aerial fighting.

It is, perhaps, significant that this self same trait was evident in the account of his early life when, as a civilian and later in uniform, Johnny met and overcame so many setbacks along the road to an eventual commission in the Royal New Zealand Air Force.

Johnny was luckier than most aspiring fighter pilots in that he was not only a natural shot, but he was also blessed with exceptional eyesight — so important to one's chances of survival in aerial combat. To succeed therefore he needed only to master the art of flying fighter aircraft, in his case the supreme Spitfire. That he succeeded is evidenced by his tally of fourteen enemy aircraft destroyed.

Johnny Checketts has secured an honoured place in the history of New Zealand airmen in World War II and he must surely rank high in the list of outstanding fighter pilots of his generation.

Alan C. Deere, DSO, OBE, DFC & Bar, RAF

# Introduction to New Edition

Twenty years after this book was first published, Johnny Checketts died peacefully at his home in Christchurch on 21 April 2006. As recently as February, when he turned 94, he seemed quite well and had even renewed his driving licence. After his beloved wife Natalie died in December 2000, he had been determined to live independently, attended in his own home by a devoted cat and regularly visited by members of his family, by old friends, neighbours and ladies who did housework and cooked some meals for him. He was none too keen, however, on visits from a variety of social workers who suggested that he abandon 16 Hudson Street (where he had lived since 1973) and move into a place more 'suitable' for a very old man. He remained cheerful and alert, gallant as ever in bantering with all his lady visitors in an old-fashioned but charmingly innocent fashion even after he was told that he had an inoperable cancer. I last saw him thirteen days before he died and there was still a twinkle in his eye.

Johnny had regularly attended St. Matthew's Anglican Church in Christchurch and held his 90th birthday party in its hall. A great many people attended and he circulated non-stop in his easy, friendly way, never sitting down for a moment and was still going strong when I left. Now, a little more than four years later, his family arranged a memorable funeral in that same church. It was really a joyful celebration of his long life. The weather was miserable, but nothing else was. The church was packed and many of those who attended – it would be wrong to call them 'mourners' – were obliged to stand at the back.

Johnny had requested that Cardinal Newman's magnificent hymn, 'Lead kindly light', be sung on this occasion. This was partly because he loved it, but mostly in memory of Agnès de la Barre de Nanteuil, one of several brave French men and women who helped him to evade the Germans and return to England after he had been forced to bale out near Abbeville on the Somme in September 1943. On his last night in her home, Agnès wrote out, in English, three verses of that hymn on a piece of paper that Johnny treasured for the rest of his life. Six months later, in March 1944, she was arrested by the Gestapo and murdered in August, aged 21.

After the service, as soon as we got outside the church, a P-51D

Mustang, laid on by the RNZAF, roared overhead. It was the last fighter-type Johnny flew and thereby paid him a fitting last tribute – paid despite low cloud and drizzle that made flying conditions marginal for such a valuable aircraft. The RNZAF also laid on a splendid Guard of Honour, together with a 'Last Post', as the hearse carried him away. We then enjoyed an excellent – and cheerful – afternoon tea, just as Johnny would have wished, though he would have been somewhat embarrassed by all the talk about his fine qualities as a husband, father, grandfather, friend and (not least) as one of the outstanding fighter pilots of the Second World War.

The first edition of this book was launched by Air Marshal David Crooks in Johnny's home town, Invercargill, on 20 February 1987, his 75th birthday. David began his career as a Pilot Officer under Johnny's command; he later played an important part in healing a rift that had opened between Johnny and the RNZAF; and Johnny was greatly moved by the warmth of his tribute. David was among the many former and present servicemen who attended his last celebration.

The launch had attracted a large, friendly turnout and two years later, in April 1989, an edited version of the book was read on national radio in ten thirty-minute episodes. Bob Parker heard these broadcasts, read the book, and decided to devote one of his popular 'This is Your Life' television shows to Johnny. Bob and I, with enthusiastic support from Natalie, successfully managed a total surprise for him, at the RNZAF Museum, Wigram, in April 1990.

The task of luring Johnny to Wigram, on the afternoon before the show, fell to me – together with the much more difficult job of persuading him to go out from a warm room onto a chilly, windswept airfield, where Bob Parker and his film crew were huddled behind a Spitfire. 'Oh, Johnny', I said, in my best hearty voice, 'there's a Spitfire. Let's go and look at it.' He refused, curtly by his standards, reminding me that he'd seen lots of Spitfires up close and felt no great urge to get cold looking at another one. Taking ruthless advantage of his good nature, I eventually persuaded him to do as I asked. There he was ambushed by Bob, agreed reluctantly to climb into the cockpit, was filmed, and allowed me to take him home. He was not best pleased, but gradually thawed (in both senses) and that evening became one of the most memorable of his life.

For the first time in 47 years he met Marie Lavenant (now van Belle). She had been traced to her home in Brittany by the television people and flown to Christchurch with her daughter Annick and son-in-law Jean-Luc. Marie was then 73. She had never before flown in an aeroplane nor left France. When Johnny and Natalie visited that country in 1976 he had telephoned her, but since he had no French and she had no English the conversation was brief and unsatisfactory. Nevertheless, Marie was gratified by his effort, because he was the only airman of all those whom she helped to escape capture who had even tried to thank her or her surviving friends in the Resistance. Marie was awarded the Croix de Guerre in 1945, but it took her family until 1980 to persuade her to accept it. 'I did so little', she told me (which isn't true), 'and others did so much more' (which may be true, but is irrelevant). Their meeting provoked floods of tears, if not many words, on both sides – though they managed to get on easy terms during the next few days, thanks to Jean-Luc, who spoke English well, and had some good laughs together about the old days.

Among other guests were Johnny's dear friend Alan Deere, flown in from England with his wife Joan. There were also several other former pilots with whom he had served, a generous selection of school friends and work mates, as well as his daughter Mary-Jane and her two children (living in Brisbane), his son David (from Invercargill) and his other son, Christopher, who lived in Christchurch with his wife Merelyn. The show attracted much favourable comment in New Zealand's press during the next few days and helped to ensure that all remaining copies of the book were sold.

Alan Deere died in 1995, deeply mourned by Johnny, but a few years later he was delighted to learn that Richard Smith had written a fine biography (*Al Deere: Wartime Fighter Pilot, Peacetime Commander*) and in May 2003 Johnny was invited by the publisher, Grub Street of London, to contribute a foreword. He later regretted not including a response he and Al often made when asked whether they were ever scared during the war. 'Not often', they said, 'only when we were flying.'

Several attempts to have my biography reprinted failed, until late last year, when I was able to tell Johnny that John Davies, of Grub Street, London, had agreed to bring out a new edition. He was, of course, delighted and from his place at the bar of that great officers' mess in the sky he can now tell Al Deere that at least he is no longer being pestered by people wishing to buy copies.

Vincent Orange,
December 2006

CHAPTER ONE

# The Road to Biggin Hill

It is difficult for anyone who was not in Fighter Command in 1943
to understand the prestige which Biggin Hill enjoyed. Its squadrons
were the Guards of the R.A.F. . . . It had the latest aircraft, famous
leaders, and the Battle of Britain's great renown. It did 'the best things
best'. . . .Biggin deserved a high standard and demanded one.
Colin Hodgkinson, *Best Foot Forward, p. 164*

The aerodrome at Biggin Hill lies about 200 metres above sea
level, set high on the North Downs, between Bromley and
Westerham, overlooking the Kentish Weald. It was still a com-
paratively rural part of West Kent in the days when Johnny
Checketts served there. The Old Jail Inn in Jail Lane was the
local pub, about a mile from the aerodrome. The White Hart,
also a favourite haunt, was at Brasted, about seven kilometres away.
During one visit there he was honoured to be asked to chalk his
signature on a large wooden blackout screen almost covered by
the signatures of pilots who flew from Biggin Hill in the Battle
of Britain and later. That screen, framed and protected by glass,
is now in the Royal Air Force Museum at Hendon.

For most of his life, Johnny has looked a good ten years younger
than his actual age. Very few of the combat pilots with whom he
served were older; most, in fact, were much younger. A coun-
tryman at heart, he has always loved either to be out of doors
— hunting or gardening — or fiddling about with machinery.
Constant activity has kept his figure slim and he still has plenty
of curly hair, though it is thinner and greyer now. But it is his

cheerful, smiling manner as much as his physical appearance that makes him seem so young. An affectionate man, he is fond of company and eager to think well of those about him. He likes a drink, especially of his home-made wine, but does not need it to put him in a good humour, nor does it makes him ponderous or maudlin. Because he is himself straightforward and un-complicated, he can easily be hurt by those who are sharper or harder. Overall, however, his sunny personality has rarely been clouded for long. He has a host of friends, many more than he realises. They know they would not seek his help or advice in vain. Nor would they think of him as a 'literary gent' and yet, one day late in 1943, soon after his return to England from seven harrow-ing weeks on the run in France, he settled down to describe a typical day at Biggin Hill during that summer. He gave his manuscript to Alan Mitchell, the New Zealand War Correspon-dent in London, and it eventually found its way into the official history of New Zealanders serving with the Royal Air Force, published in the 1950s. It is by far the longest quotation from a single pilot in that massive work.

Johnny's day, as he recalled it, began beautifully, still and warm. The sun was dispersing a light ground mist, leaving the hawthorne and blackberry bushes smelling fresh and clean as he strolled from the mess shortly before 6 a.m. to attend a briefing by Alan Deere, his friend and mentor. He felt pleased with life that fine morning. Mail from New Zealand had just arrived; the operation outlined by Alan promised intense excitement; the Spitfires, so 'sleek and pretty' (in his eyes) seemed eager to be off and even the drab air-field buildings looked familiar and comfortable. Best of all, the pilots under his command were laughing and joking as they chang-ed into flying kit. He marvelled as he listened at their perfect fellowship and privately wished he could always be in such grand company.

When he had strapped himself into his cockpit and checked his instruments and controls, he looked across at Alan's Spitfire. They exchanged cheery waves and then, for a few minutes, there was nothing to do. This was always the worst time, waiting and trying not to think. Suddenly Alan started his engine, the signal for twenty-three other pilots to do the same. Johnny watched him move slowly away, followed by the eleven aircraft of the squadron he was leading that day. The Spitfires formed up line abreast and took off amid a tremendous noise that Johnny scarcely noticed, he was so busy leading his own squadron into position for take-off. A last look round. As usual, the station doctor, adjutant and intelligence officer were watching the fighters depart, together with the ground crews. He waved his hand both in farewell and as a signal to his pilots. Opening the throttle, he felt a familiar exhilaration as the Spitfire surged powerfully forward. Soon his squadron was climbing over the grey-green fields of Kent, taking position behind and down sun of Alan's Spitfires. Johnny quickly checked his gunsight, gun safety catches, oxygen, wireless and petrol. By then the Channel coast was already in sight and so too were the twin-engined Mitchell bombers which the Spitfires were to escort to targets in France.

Johnny ordered his pilots to take up their battle formation and begin that ceaseless, systematic search of the sky upon which depended their lives and those of the bomber crews far below. But no enemy aircraft appeared. Too early for Huns? Perhaps they're waiting to pick us off on the way home when we're tired and careless? How often can one tell the boys — and oneself — to relax only on the ground, back at dear old Biggin? Alan's voice broke radio silence, calling a turn to starboard. The formation reached its target unmolested and Johnny saw a spatter of bomb bursts throwing up clouds of dust and smoke. Then came the flak and he climbed hastily away. Flak was no danger to tiny fighters, flying fast and high — or so some people said, though not usually when their aircraft were being buffetted by shells bursting near them. Alan called another turn. The flak fell behind and the French coast drew near. Many German aircraft were reported airborne, but none approached this formation. Kent was awake now: Johnny could see smoke rising from chimneys in factories, towns and villages even before he crossed the white cliffs. The bombers made their own way home from the English coast and the Spitfire pilots dived swiftly towards Biggin Hill and a second breakfast. Afterwards, he and Alan lazed in the mid-morning sun, discussing the show and chattering away like children. For a time their only concern was to keep Johnny's dog Winkle away from his precious tomato plants.

Alan decided to brief the pilots for a second show at noon.

While he was deep in conversation with the intelligence officer, Johnny seized the chance for a chat with 'Sailor' Malan. An even more famous fighter pilot than Alan Deere, Sailor was then station commander at Biggin Hill and, like Alan, a good friend and mentor to Johnny. They talked about aircraft, the morning's show and shotguns until Alan started his briefing. It was as usual very thorough, leaving no-one in doubt about what he was required to do. Johnny liked to watch his pilots' faces during briefings. All were tense, of course, but some looked keen, others sombre; only a few were able to appear unconcerned. After the briefing, everyone went to the bar for a beer before lunch. Johnny took his out on to the lawn for a few peaceful moments, gazing over the soft green fields and distant woodlands, views of which he never tired. He made himself eat a little lunch, more to fill in time than because he wanted anything to eat on such a warm day. Down at the dispersal hut, the usual bedlam was building up. New records had been found for the radiogram and everyone was suddenly very busy and noisy. Pilots were looking for mislaid bits of gear or consulting each other about places on their maps and details of the briefing; fitters and riggers were discussing repairs made to particular aircraft and telephones were ringing constantly.

Alan and Johnny sat quietly in the sun until the other pilots were in their machines. For this operation, Alan decided to lead Johnny's squadron and Johnny therefore led a section of four fighters. As always, he checked and re-checked his cockpit instruments and controls during the interminable wait for take-off, a wait made worse this day by the unusual heat. Getting airborne again was a great relief. The operation, however, proved uneventful: the bombers turned up on time, everyone evaded the coastal flak (both going out and coming home) and the target was accurately found and evidently hit; its local flak did no harm and the Luftwaffe failed to appear. Safely back at Biggin Hill, he could find no good reason not to catch up on office work. That done, he joined some fellow enthusiasts ready to practise clay bird shooting and lay small wagers on their skill. Tea — hot, strong and sweet — was served at 4 p.m. and Johnny, lying at ease on the grass, convinced himself that there would be no more flying that day. He threw a stick for Winkle to retrieve a few times and then fell to thinking about his home in Invercargill and happy days duck shooting in the New River estuary. He thought about his girl friend in Christchurch and old friends scattered around the world, fighting either the Germans or the Japanese. Such thoughts led to no happy conclusion, so Johnny decided to shower, change and go out for the evening. No sooner was he ready, wearing his best uniform, than orders came for a third operation, take-off at 6 p.m.

This time there was an encounter with the Luftwaffe. Turning with their bombers away from the target, Johnny spotted several specks in the sky far to port. They closed rapidly and he was soon able to call Alan on his radio and tell him that he had fourteen Focke-Wulf 190s in sight, all making for the bombers. Johnny's squadron was in an excellent position to intercept and minutes later the Spitfires were among the German fighters, engaging their whole attention and thus enabling the bombers to make good their escape. He got on the tail of one fighter at close range, close enough to see the black crosses on each wing clearly before firing a two-second burst of cannon shells into its fuselage. Smoke and flame gushed out and the fighter spun away. Johnny gave it no further attention. Instead, supported by his wingman (guardian of his tail) he chased after another Focke-Wulf which had rolled over on to its back and dived down vertically. The three machines went down at very high speeds, Johnny closing the range slightly and firing whenever he had a chance. Eventually he hit his enemy's starboard wing and closed the range to two hundred metres as the aircraft levelled out just above the ground. The Focke-Wulf fled inland and, though he drew closer, his cannon jammed and he had to rely on machine-gun fire. He saw bullets strike home and a thin white trail of smoke appear, gradually turning black. But he and his wingman, realising they were being drawn ever farther from the coast, broke away and set course for England at ground level. French peasants waved to them and Johnny, though wet with perspiration and gasping for breath, was thrilled by their response and the knowledge that one or two Germans would trouble them no more. He maintained maximum speed all the way to the Channel, looking about for more aircraft, friendly or enemy, but seeing none. So ended another day of the sharpest contrasts: at one moment idly sipping tea in Kent, at another fighting for his life high over France.

Johnny had first visited Biggin Hill early in 1942 while stationed at Kenley, about eight kilometres to the west. The damage done during the Battle of Britain was still plainly visible: several buildings had been extensively repaired, others were obviously new and many bomb craters in a valley west of the airfield had not been filled in. He read all he could find on Biggin Hill, spoke to men and women who served there and wished he could join them. When he did join them, from January to September 1943, the spirit was the finest he ever encountered in the Service, among ground staff as well as pilots. Moreover, that aerodrome was set in such a lovely part of England. 'On a fine day,' he wrote, 'Biggin Hill was a wonderland, even in wartime: surrounded by beautiful farms and houses with hedgerows that were so neat and attractive.' When he was not on duty, he would often roam the nearby fields and lanes looking for partridge or simply enjoying the fresh air and scenery.

On 19 September 1943, two weeks after Johnny was shot down over northern France, a Chapel of Remembrance dedicated to St George was opened in a disused army hut to commemorate in particular the deeds of those who fought at Biggin Hill during the Battle of Britain. When he returned to England after many exciting and frightening adventures in France, he gave thanks in that chapel for his safe deliverance. It was destroyed by fire in December 1946, but a larger and grander chapel was built during the next few years and dedicated by the Bishop of Rochester in November 1951. Although a graceful and dignified memorial, well worthy of those whom it commemorates, it can never quite replace the first humble building in the hearts of those who knew it. Twelve stained glass windows commemorate the squadrons which once flew from Biggin Hill; one window, given anonymously, bears that inexpressibly moving inscription: 'And some there be who have no memorial.' 453 pilots of 52 squadrons flying from the Biggin Hill Sector lost their lives in World War II and a Book of Remembrance recalls them in Stephen Spender's words:

> They travelled a short while
> Toward the sun
> And left the vivid air
> Signed with their honour

A quotation from Psalm 62 is embroidered on the altar frontlet: 'In the shadow of Thy wings will I rejoice.' Outside the chapel stand a Hurricane and a Spitfire, immortal aircraft whose images are fixed for ever in the minds of those who served at Biggin Hill or any other fighter station in Britain or elsewhere. They are fixed as firmly in the minds of those who honour the men and women who built or tended or flew them.

Johnny Checketts remains very proud of his connection with that station: 'Biggin Hill,' he says, 'was like a home to me in the Royal Air Force and I will always look upon it with the greatest affection.' He will show friends his Biggin Hill tie (worn only on special occasions): it is coloured light blue for the sky, white for the Cliffs of Dover and green for the fields of Kent. The station badge — a sword unsheathed and pointing upwards to fend off attack from above — appears surrounded by a chain representing the ring of Royal Air Force stations which then defended London. The motto, *The Strongest Link*, refers to the fact that the Biggin Hill Sector claimed well over 1,000 victories in aerial combat during World War II, by far the most in Fighter Command.

Johnny took part in the famous action which brought about the thousandth victory and the still more famous celebrations which followed. But ten months earlier, in July 1942, the 900 mark had been reached. Three pewter tankards were made and suitably inscribed, one for the confirmed victories, one for the probables and one for those enemy aircraft damaged. They were presented to the Officers' Mess and during 1943 Johnny often drank from the 'damaged' tankard. When the Mess was broken up, Group Captain North (formerly a fighter controller) acquired this tankard and left it to his son John, an Air Training Corps cadet at Biggin Hill in 1943 who used to wash down the Spitfires. John North became a merchant seaman and visited New Zealand in the sixties, meeting Johnny once again at Port Chalmers, Dunedin. He had the tankard with him and Johnny enjoyed the pleasure of drinking out of it once more. When North returned as master of the *Cumberland* in February 1972, Johnny was invited aboard at Port Chalmers and, to his great surprise and delight, that tankard was presented to him. It remains one of his most precious possessions.

In an interview with a Christchurch journalist in 1977, Johnny was asked what it felt like to shoot down an aircraft. 'I was always conscious,' he replied, 'that there was a man in it who loved someone and was loved by someone. Yet in an odd sort of way I enjoyed the fighting because I was good at it, even though I was scared. And when the war was over, you felt let down, as though there was nothing left. You had been trained at it and you were good at it and it was all you knew how to do properly. You know, they were great days in a way. In the life of every man there is a peak. I often think that mine was during the war.' If that is true, the peak came in 1943, during his year at Biggin Hill.

The Royal Air Force ceased to fly from there in January 1958 and it became a selection centre for air and ground personnel. The airfield is now occupied by a civil airport for business and club flying. Once a year, in May, its great days are recalled when an International Air Fair is held. By 1978, some senior officers in the Royal New Zealand Air Force believed it high time that Johnny was given an opportunity to return to Biggin Hill. The Chief of Air Staff, Air Vice-Marshal Laurence Siegert, therefore invited him to attend the fair that year as his personal representative. Johnny's wife Natalie was unable to accompany him (her mother was then critically ill and would in fact die while he was away) but she urged him to go. He flew from Auckland in a Lockheed Hercules, thoroughly enjoying the week-long journey and spending many hours on the flight deck of that 'mighty aeroplane'.

The Hercules landed in England at Brize Norton, Oxfordshire, where he helped to wash and polish it for the honour of the Royal New Zealand Air Force. This job was not quite finished before it was time to fly on to 'dear old Biggin'. He sat with one of the navigators giving him the courses to take them south of the air-field, over the Oxted chalk-pit — a favourite landmark — and down on to the long main runway. Approaching and landing at Biggin Hill for the first time in more than thirty years were wonderful experiences for Johnny, though little on the ground remained the same. They parked the Hercules opposite the Alsace Squadron's dispersal (now occupied by an aero club), got out their buckets and mops and soon had the Hercules sparkling all over. He overheard one man say: 'Fancy seeing officers washing an aeroplane; that would never do for the RAF.' But Johnny was as proud of 'our beautiful machine' as the rest of the crew and only too happy to lend a hand even though he was then sixty-six years old.

He was interviewed by the BBC and some newspapermen and then accommodated in an hotel in Bromley (over which he had flown and fought numerous times and within which he had sometimes relaxed with comrades now long dead). Terry Gardiner, a member of the Hercules' crew, recalled that he had been appalled by the prospect of interviews and 'vehemently denied that he was a fighter ace'. But the sound of a Merlin engine as a Spitfire IX warmed up relaxed him and there were tears in his eyes as he watched it take off. He had taken to introducing three young members of the crew as his sons and when a barmaid asked why only one was red-haired, he replied: 'Because he's the oldest; I was rusty the first time.' During the next two days he visited the chapel and had the pleasure of seeing many wartime aircraft in motion, if not in action, as well as machines unconceived of in 1943. He saw some special friends again — the Fergusons of Oxted, Alan Deere and his wife at Wendover — but time ran out all too soon. Alan drove him to Brize Norton, where the Hercules awaited. Every member of the crew welcomed the opportunity to meet Alan, and Johnny was thrilled to see that his friend's magnificent war-time achievements were still remembered. The Hercules took off next morning and Johnny, watching England fall away, wondered if he would ever visit that country again. He reached home safely, a beautifully-maintained house in Christchurch named, of course, Biggin Hill.

## CHAPTER TWO

# Dreaming of Flying: February 1912 to October 1940

John Milne Checketts is from Invercargill. It is the world's most southerly city and lies near the south coast of New Zealand's South Island. He was born there on 20 February 1912 in his parents' home at 32 Woodhouse Street. His father's parents were unknown to him, but his mother's were of Irish and Scottish origin: his grandmother, Margaret Forde, arriving in New Zealand from County Cork in 1861; his grandfather, David Milne, from Aberdeenshire a year later. David and his two brothers settled in Southland, where they worked as agricultural contractors and road makers. A patriotic Scot, David could recite Burns by the hour and Johnny still has some of his books. David and Margaret met in Queenstown, married in Invercargill and remained deeply attached to each other for the rest of their hard-working lives.

Johnny's mother (Mary Jane) was the second of their five children and married Ernest Matthew Checketts in 1911. They had three children, of whom Johnny was the eldest. Mary Jane was a good wife to her husband, a loving mother and (not least among Johnny's many happy memories of her) a marvellous cook. His sister, christened Margaret Victoria but always known as Peggy, had a strong and independent character. Encouraged by her mother, she learned to play the piano very well and gradually acquired an excellent collection of books. The third child, Ernest Alan, was such a live wire that he was nicknamed Ginger even though his hair was dark.

Ernest Checketts was a carrier in and around Invercargill, keeping a dray and two horses. It was heavy work and he spent much of his day amid dust or mud, for there were no sealed roads in Southland then. He also leased some land near his home on which he kept a couple of cows and a few chickens. Ernest was very good with animals and birds and often won prizes at shows. On one famous occasion he won a pepper tin half-filled with fine gold dust. It was the first gold Johnny ever saw but, though he never forgot that thrilling moment, he was not inspired to seek his own; gold has no dominion over him. He remembers the shingle laid in the town's very wide main streets as some sort of answer to mud or dust. Better still, he remembers the old horse-drawn tramcars, replaced in 1912 by electric cars and dumped on waste ground near the estuary. There they provided generations of local children with a wonderful adventure playground.

Johnny's first home was built on a long, narrow quarter-acre section between Woodhouse Street and the Invercargill-Tokanui railway line. In those days it was known as the Appleby railway because it passed through a nearby station of that name. The gradient was quite steep thereabouts and the trains used to pass very slowly, closely observed by the three Checketts children who would sometimes put a penny on the track to see what would happen to it. Pennies being none too plentiful, this was not a pastime of which their father approved. Johnny was very happy at home, for love was never in short supply even though money might be. His mother liked to read aloud or play the violin, his father played the piano and everyone would sing songs, loudly and cheerfully, if not especially tunefully. Two of the family's most prized possessions, from Johnny's point of view, were a boisterous little dog called Ponty and a somewhat battered tricycle owned by each child in turn. Even though the section contained fruit trees, and gooseberry and blackcurrant bushes, there was still plenty of room to play.

Johnny's education began at Invercargill South School in 1917, when he was five. It was then one of the country's largest primary schools and many of its pupils have made their mark in New

Zealand society. Among them, E. R. Wilson, an architect responsible for some notable buildings in Invercargill; Billy Stead, vice-
captain of a famous rugby team, the 1905 All Blacks; Sir Thomas
Macdonald, a High Commissioner for New Zealand in London;
and Alex Lindsay, a violinist and conductor who enjoyed an international reputation. Johnny's mother had dressed him specially for his first day, squeezing him into an Eton collar which he
hated exceedingly and wore only under the loudest protest of which
his lungs were capable. His teacher, Miss E. W. Bellamy, was 'a
sweet lady' who taught at the school for twenty years and left a
legacy to pay for a statue dedicated to the children of Invercargill
which stands by Coronation Avenue, near the Feldwick Gates.
He liked her poems and stories, sang lustily whenever invited
(sometimes when not) and displayed a talent for folding paper
into elaborate patterns: he has always loved to use his hands. His
sister Peggy started school on Armistice Day in November 1918,
a day Johnny would never forget because at about 10 a.m. the
Headmaster, Mr James Hain, came into the classroom and sent
all the children home. Peggy, unlike Johnny, was most reluctant
to leave. He had to lead her by the hand all the way, a distance
of over a mile. It was raining hard and she was screaming with
rage at having her first school day ruined.

Johnny vividly recalls the great influenza epidemic then sweeping
through the world which reached Invercargill in November 1918.
The death rate in Southland was proportionately higher than in
any other part of New Zealand and Johnny's parents took on much
extra work, cooking and delivering food to their friends and
neighbours, visiting the sick and doing what they could to comfort them. No member of the Checketts family died, but at the
height of the epidemic Johnny's beloved grandfather, David Milne,
whom he always thought of as 'a magnificent old Highlander',
suffered a fatal heart attack. No sooner had the epidemic passed
away than Johnny lost his almost equally beloved home in
Woodhouse Street. His father decided to sell it and buy a small
farm just south of Kew Hospital, on the way to Clifton. The farm,
all twenty acres of it, lay on the eastern side of the New River
estuary, an important meeting-place for whalers and sealers in
New Zealand's early European history. Johnny grew to love it,
playing in the water, fishing the creeks and learning to swim in

deep, warm pools at a place called Shellbanks, about three kilometres south of the farm. He and his friends had to go through rushes and over flood banks to get there, but they were spared the need to wear swimming trunks because none of the local girls were prepared to wade and scramble so far simply for a swim. After his swim, Johnny would bring home flour bags full of the shells which were so abundant there, as grit for the family's chickens.

Another memorable event of those days was the return of the first soldiers from service overseas. Johnny was taken by his father in the dray to see them arrive in pouring rain at the railway station, where a great crowd gave them a tumultuous welcome. Child though he still was, he sensed the overwhelming emotion of that occasion and would experience it again, a generation later, when he himself received the same hero's welcome in the same rain at the same station. The peace celebrations in Invercargill in July 1919 were spectacular. Johnny's father took the whole family to see the procession of horse-drawn floats through the streets. One float was done up to resemble a tank: a mighty, lumbering thing which he saw clearly (mounted on his father's shoulders) and remembered vividly, though it did not inspire him to join an armoured regiment in the next war. In March 1920, aged eight, he saw his first aeroplane: an Avro 504K, flown low over the town, tantalisingly close, by Captain Euan Dickson of the Canterbury Aviation Company. The town's factory whistles gave Dickson 'a salvo' (reported the *Southland Times*) as he circled overhead. Landing on the racecourse, he completed 'the first journey of a modern aeroplane from Christchurch to Invercargill'. As with the returning soldiers, this memory would be revived for Johnny a generation later when he made the first flight in a jet aircraft over Invercargill, attracting the same excited attention as had Dickson.

School was more than five kilometres from the Checketts' home and until their father could afford to buy them bicycles the children often had to walk there and back. When the weather was particularly bad — that is, wet as well as windy — he might take them in the dray, but not always because his working day began so early. The gravel roads were a trial on foot or wheels, but their mother produced piles of wonderful hot buttered scones for them to come home to. Johnny became a Boy Scout and quickly learned to love and respect New Zealand's beautiful countryside (for many years in later life, it would be part of his job to help protect it). He was an active boy, keen on games — rugby and cricket especially — and, for a while, fascinated by marbles and kite-flying. By now, his father had seven Jersey cows (pure-bred but unregistered) and some prize Tamworth pigs of which he was very proud. There were also ducks and chickens and all the farmyard clutter that so fascinates children.

About this time, Ernest Checketts bought a brand-new motor-car: a black Model T Ford. Although an excellent driver of horse-drawn vehicles, he had never before been behind the wheel of a horseless carriage. Nevertheless, he got the car started and mobile, encouraged by the man who was supposed to be his instructor. Together, they got as far as the instructor's home without incident and Ernest thereupon attempted to reach his own home solo. He got safely to the Appleby Hotel, where there was a water trough at which he was accustomed to refresh his horses. He called 'Whoah', but the car failed to respond and instead collided firmly with the trough while doing a brisk 25 k.p.h. The radiator was forced back over the engine and he was left to complete the journey home on foot, much to his own annoyance and the intense disappointment of his children, eagerly looking forward to the sight of their father rolling grandly up to the door in a magnificent new Ford. Neither then nor later did he find the incident at all amusing; the more so, perhaps, because for years afterwards the horse trough displayed the evidence of his embarrassment only too plainly.

In 1926, when he was fourteen, Johnny went to Southland Technical College, obtained his Certificate of Proficiency and took engineering courses which he continued at evening classes after leaving the college in August 1928. He was already fascinated by machinery of all kinds and did well in practical work: an understanding of engines, machine tools, blacksmith work and carpentry came easily to him, but academic subjects usually found him wanting. The Rector, Mr C. A. Stewart, hammered him unmercifully and was not impressed even when he came top of the whole college in English. He was summoned to the rostrum at assembly where Stewart coldly announced his triumph. No word of praise, not even a smile. Johnny does not remember him with affection. His first job on leaving college was with his uncle, Jack

Checketts, a plasterer and tiler. Uncle Jack, however, was 'a tyrant of the first order', in Johnny's opinion, and he soon walked out on him, braving not only Jack's anger but even his father's. He found himself a much better job as an apprentice mechanic with G. W. Woods & Co., motor engineers and Ford agents in Invercargill. He loved the job 'dirty and all as it was'.

Aeroplanes were now to be seen more frequently over the town, but each one was still an event in Johnny's life. He did not then suppose that he would ever be a pilot himself; only supermen, he thought, could cope with such magnificent machines. In January 1933, however, the famous aviator Sir Charles Kingsford Smith began a tour of New Zealand in his huge Fokker tri-motor monoplane, the *Southern Cross*. His visit to Myross Bush aerodrome (north of Invercargill) early in March was eagerly awaited by practically everyone in Southland. Special trains and buses carried most of the 6,000 spectators who went to see Smithy and his great aeroplane. There were also flying displays by six de Havilland Gipsy Moths of the Southland and Otago aero clubs and, that evening, a special screening of *Air Mail,* Universal's great epic of the air, a film brought by Kingsford Smith from Australia to New Zealand. Johnny was thrilled by the sight of *Southern Cross* in the air and on the ground, actually in his own home town. Joyrides were on offer, but only at the enormous cost of ten shillings a time and so he had to content himself with watching and wanting. It was then that he, like so many other New Zealanders of his generation, first began to dream of flying; he would master this wonderful skill if ever he got a chance.

Meanwhile, he took up rowing and sailing — demanding sports requiring, as did flying, strength and fitness. The club captain of his rowing club, Russell Bagrie, was also the amateur middleweight boxing champion of New Zealand and encouraged Johnny to take up boxing as part of a training programme. Many professional boxers used to train in the rowing club shed and Johnny sometimes sparred with them. On one occasion, he flew angrily at an opponent who promptly knocked him flat. Neither he nor his opponent took the incident amiss and were always good friends afterwards, but Johnny took care to keep his temper in check. He began to travel outside his home town, as far as Queenstown and Dunedin, to take part in rowing and sailing competitions.

He also took up golf with his cousin and good friend, Jack Milne.
Johnny had long been keen on shooting, either water fowl or
clay targets. He was taught to shoot at the age of fifteen by Adam
Mahar, an elderly friend of the family. An educated man who
spoke English beautifully, Adam had once been intended for the
priesthood, but a fondness for drink and wrestling jointly ended
those hopes. He was big and strong and had a rare gift for dealing
with sick animals. Whenever there was heavy or dirty work to
be done around the farm, Adam was always at hand, getting on
with it cheerfully and competently. Johnny loved him dearly and
paid the closest attention to his instructions in all matters concern-
ing the proper use and care of guns. During the open season,
Johnny and his friend Joe Pasco spent many happy hours hunting
both duck and godwit. In January and February, they would lie
in the warm sands of the Invercargill Estuary, decoying the fast-
flying godwits into their sights. The Waihopai River flowed into
the estuary about half a kilometre behind the Invercargill Post
Office. All that land, now reclaimed, was then an ideal place for
godwits to feed. Johnny and Joe would sometimes drift down upon
them in a dinghy and shoot them as they took flight. About ten
were needed for a pie, he recalls: 'they were delicious; tender
as chicken, but much more tasty.' In those years, he learned to
see and hit a small moving target; skills which he would later put
to more serious use. As Johnnie Johnson, the highest scoring Allied
fighter pilot of World War II would write: 'The outstanding fighter
pilots, on both sides, were outdoor types — game shots, hunters,
ball players — who knew about range, timing and lead.'

He had scraped together enough money for a motor cycle by
about 1930 and began to enter competitions, hill climbs and sand
races. Although a frequent winner, the prizes were too small to
cover expenses: for instance, a racing spark plug cost thirty shillings whereas twenty shillings was a typical first prize. Johnny
therefore decided to see what could be done with a standard plug,
second grade petrol and careful tuning — and won as many prizes
as before. Even after half a century, Johnny's reputation as a daring and successful competitor in motor cycle races on a grass track
at Rugby Park, Invercargill, is very much alive, as the present
writer knows from the number of letters sent to him by men and
women who remember Johnny as 'a wild one, a real daredevil',

a great favourite with the crowds as much for his spectacular falls as his frequent victories. He seemed completely fearless and more than one correspondent has suggested that the explanation of his later fame as a fighter pilot lies here.

During the years between 1929 and 1935, New Zealand suffered severe economic depression. Ernest Checketts had to sell his horses and take on a paper run that was soon lost. The family was reduced to living entirely off the farm, eked out by the small wages of Johnny and Peggy (Alan was still at school), but everyone pulled together and they struggled through, selling milk, butter, eggs and pork. Johnny completed his apprenticeship in September 1934 and worked for three different motor dealers during the next five years, all of whom found him a model employee. In 1936 he became an A Grade mechanic 'of exceptional ability . . . clean and tidy in his work, and sober in habits' (according to one reference) and his wages went up twopence an hour; for a forty-hour week he earned good money, four pounds eighteen shillings and, he wrote, 'revelled in the work'. Fifty years later, George Sutherland — a fellow mechanic — clearly remembers his exceptional skill, his generosity, his love of the outdoors, his determination to become a fighter pilot as war threatened and, above all, what *fun* he was to work with.

Johnny enjoyed his first and only pre-war flight in the summer of 1937-8 when Fred Adams, a pilot and engineer with the Southland Aero Club, took him aloft for a few exhilarating minutes in the club's de Havilland Puss Moth. Although Johnny could not afford to take up flying seriously and Fred was unable to give him another free flight, those unforgettable minutes fuelled his imagination and he dreamed more than ever of flying. In August 1939, 'having undertaken to join the Royal New Zealand Air Force in the event of war', he was enrolled in the Civil Reserve. The Air Department in Wellington was naturally keen to have him as a ground mechanic and told him that without matriculation he would have no chance of becoming a pilot. But Johnny was determined not to spend the war doing what he had done in peacetime. This, he thought, was his great — and last — chance to break out of the familiar mould and try something totally new. Even though he was already twenty-seven, his ambition was to serve as a fighter pilot: one of the most physically demanding, dangerous and exciting duties that the war would require.

The Air Department sympathised and set up a course of twenty-one educational assignments. The course was taught in Invercargill by Dr George Uttley, Rector of Southland Boys High School. Johnny and other aspirants attended two evening classes a week, plunging into a world of Arithmetic, Algebra, Trigonometry, Electricity, Navigation and Morse Code which was at first quite beyond his grasp. Refusing to despair, however, he bought elementary textbooks covering these subjects and struggled desperately far into the night in an effort to master the basic principles. 'I've never known anyone so keen to get away,' recalls one old school friend. 'He studied so hard to make the grade.' Jack Milne used to call him 'Richthofen', but behind the banter Johnny recognised how keen Jack was to see him achieve his ambition. This was a bad time for Johnny because in August 1939 his dearly-loved mother had died, aged only fifty-eight. Yet somehow he completed the assignments, though scraping through them with nothing to spare. He was well aware that he must fail if the Air Force were to examine him more thoroughly, so he applied to the Air Department for a correspondence course covering those assignments — and remains grateful for its ready agreement to provide this course. He found that he now began to master them more comfortably, partly because he preferred to work alone at his own pace.

The war having now begun, the young men of Invercargill, like their fathers before them, were leaving for training camps before going overseas. His brother Alan had volunteered to join the army as a gunner and was training at Ngaruawahia, near Auckland. The manager of the garage where Johnny worked (Macaulay Motors) called him into the office shortly after the outbreak of war and told him that he was fired. It was nothing personal, he said, but business was likely to fall off and since Johnny was the only single man in a team of eight, he would have to go even though no other A Grade mechanic was employed. This was the first and only time in his life that he was dismissed and the memory still rankles. Ten days later, however, he was asked to return because business had suddenly boomed. He agreed, but on his own terms: he would continue to help his father on the farm during the day and work at the garage each evening — at overtime rates. Sadly, his small triumph was soured by the actions of some malicious person or persons in the town: because he was conspicuously still at home, so many white feathers were posted to him, he remembers, 'that I could have stuffed a pillow with them'. He therefore wrote to the Air Department, pointing out that men had been accepted for aircrew training since he applied and asking why he was still waiting. Within the week he was in the Air Force.

CHAPTER THREE

# Learning to Fly:
# October 1940
# to November 1941

Late in October 1940 Johnny left Invercargill by train with fifteen
other Southland recruits on the first stage of his journey to Levin,
north of Wellington, where he would receive four weeks' primary
training. He was glad to get away for several reasons: Britain seemed
then in grave danger of defeat by Nazi Germany and he was anxious to get into the fight; he missed both his mother and his
brother; his friends had all left and, not least, he had never before
been out of the South Island.

The journey to Levin was a sore trial — thirty hours by train
and ferry — but he and the other aspiring pilots, navigators and
air gunners found little rest there. Long, hard hours were spent
on the parade ground, being drilled by grim-faced corporals. As
well as inculcating instant obedience, however, the staff at Levin
paid plenty of attention to teaching essential skills, such as an
understanding of the principles of flight, methods of navigation
and the use of weapons. For nearly three weeks he had no official
number (it had not reached Levin from Wellington) and, consequently, no service dress. He had to handwash his only two shirts,
which became scruffier and scruffier, and wear his suit — 'a jolly
good one it was too' — all day and every day until it was crumpled
almost beyond recovery and stank of stale sweat from the long

sessions on the parade ground under a hot summer sun. More important, he found the lectures interesting and, to his surprise, did very well in the tests which were held frequently. His private fears that he would not be able to cope with the work on the ground — let alone in the air — began to evaporate.

From Levin, he returned to the South Island: to Taieri, near Dunedin, where he arrived on 25 November and enjoyed his first service flight next day. Taieri was the home of No. 1 Elementary Flying Training School, using bright yellow de Havilland Tiger Moths; hundreds of them, he thought, all wonderful. Group Captain Duncan Smith (an outstanding British fighter pilot, decorated five times) would describe the Tiger Moth as 'a great aeroplane that required to be flown the whole time and found you out if you were wanting in any of the basic skills.' Johnny agreed wholeheartedly. He promptly fell in love with that aeroplane and, despite suffering love's usual frustrations and anxieties, is still faithful to it after more than forty years. Not only were there real live aeroplanes at Taieri, but the flying equipment was of high quality and even the food was plentiful and excellent. Sadly, many of the instructors (drawn from civilian aero clubs) were bored and restless. They had little desire to continue in wartime work they had done in peacetime and Johnny sympathised — more deeply, perhaps, after he left Taieri than while he was there. He had five instructors in his first nine hours in the air and each one told him to do things differently. Not surprisingly, he was soon confused and depressed. Even the successful completion of his first solo, on 17 December 1940, did little to lift his spirits.

Harry Lett, his flight commander, was an elderly man who often seemed unwell and, perhaps in consequence, was either sharp-tongued or gloomily silent. On one occasion, shortly after Johnny had successfully completed his first shaky solo, he was required to fly with Lett for a blind-flying test. Johnny climbed into the rear cockpit and pulled over the hood. While taxying out to take-off, he suddenly decided that he could no longer stand Lett's surly manner. He leaned forward into the gosport tube and said: 'You know Sir, I hate flying with you.' A moment later, the throttle was snapped out of his hand and Lett taxied smartly back to the hangar, climbed out and disappeared without a word.

Another instructor, Pilot Officer Bob Penniket, asked what was

going on. Johnny poured out his sad tale and said he was going
to hand in his flying gear and join the army; he had no friends
here, he was never going to make a proper pilot and was heartily
sick of being messed about. Bob listened sympathetically, calmed
him down and said that he would himself take over his instruction, starting from scratch. He discussed flying problems in detail
with him while on the ground and for the first time Johnny began
to feel he might master them. 'I only found out some time later,'
wrote Bob in October 1985, 'that he was listed for grounding and
came to me as a last resort . . . he had been pretty uptight when
he came to me but relaxed as time went on.' Even so, Johnny
left Taieri after eight weeks with a Below Average rating as a pilot
from Flight Lieutenant Lett. Among the special faults which must
be watched, Lett noted that Johnny was 'forgetful which way to
turn on to courses'. His flying career, then, got off to a less than
brilliant start, but without Bob Penniket's friendly interest — even
more than his skilful tuition — it would have ended there and then.

On 18 January 1941, with fifty-one flying hours to his credit
(twenty-four of them solo), he was sent to No. 1 Service Flying
Training School at Wigram, near Christchurch. Apart from six
hours dual instruction in an Avro 626, he flew the Fairey Gordon,
a huge biplane (in comparison to the tiny Tiger Moth) with
a 525 horse power Armstrong Siddeley Panther engine that was
four times as powerful. Because of its size and the absence of wheel
brakes, it was a difficult machine to handle on the ground. But
in the air, 'it was a very gentle aircraft, quite a delight to fly'.
He quickly realised, however, that the Gordon was reserved for
the lowly-rated pilots; the best flew the Airspeed Oxford, a modern
twin-engined monoplane. Johnny was obliged to swallow his disappointment and try to improve his standing. After nearly five
hours in the Gordon, he was sent solo on 23 January by Fred
Adams, the man who gave him his first flight in 1935. Fred was
now 'a fairly irrascible' instructor. But it was with weapons that
Johnny made his first real mark as an airman: 'The Browning,
Lewis and Vickers machine-guns were a joy to me,' he recalled,
'and I must say that I revelled in this subject.' He was top of his
class, obtaining ninety-nine marks out of a hundred, losing one
mark for calling an aeroplane 'she'.

While stationed at Wigram, he was able to visit his mother's sister, his aunt Annie, who lived in Riccarton Road opposite the Bush Inn. She had a large family — seven boys and three girls. Jack Milne was then training nearby at Burnham Military Camp with other friends from the south and so Johnny was able to feel very much at home — at weekends. One weekend he met Jack as usual in Christchurch, although he had a raging headache and felt distinctly unwell. He wanted to return quietly to Wigram and rest, but Jack persuaded him to go to a party. There he met a young Christchurch schoolteacher, one Natalie Grover, whose smiles swiftly cured his headache. He spent most of the evening talking to her and took her home afterwards. He telephoned her the next evening and thereafter they saw each other or at least talked to each other as often as possible. During this time, he experienced the delicious anguish of balancing another few minutes with Natalie against the tedium of an endless walk to Wigram, should he miss the last tram. One day, while she was teaching, a biplane flew low over her school, waggling its wings. Children and teachers alike were entranced and wondered what was going on. Natalie smiled and said nothing.

On 7 March, however, the day before his wings examination, an incident occurred which took his mind off Natalie entirely. He broke a bone in his right foot at physical training exercises and was immediately plastered up to the knee and sent on six weeks' leave. The accident gravely disturbed him because he had just turned twenty-nine and was acutely aware that very few fighter pilots in any of the world's air forces were as old as he. If he failed to get his wings soon, he might never get them; at best, he would spend the war in New Zealand as an instructor. He could not settle at home, what with his worries over his future, his desire to keep in touch with Natalie and — not least — the discomfort of crutches. He returned early to Wigram where Jim Maxwell, one of the cooks, still remembers him hobbling about. 'He was a nice chap,' thought Jim, 'always helpful to the kitchen staff.' Perhaps it was because he had an insatiable passion for baked potatoes. At last, on 3 May, he took his wings examination, but was rated no better than average as a pilot. This examination marked the end of his intermediate flying training and he then progressed to the Advanced Training School at Wigram where the work, though still in the Gordon, was purely military. He practised formation flying, high dive and low level bombing, air-to-ground machine gunning and several navigation exercises, among them a solo flight from Wigram to Blenheim in Marlborough via Cape Campbell and back to Wigram, a total distance of some 300 nautical miles.

Quite apart from meeting Natalie Grover, Johnny enjoyed his time at Wigram. The training was extremely good, he thought, and carefully planned. He was especially happy in the Advanced Training School, where the supervision was less strict and one spent longer in the air, practising tasks which he knew would soon be matters of life and death for himself and others. When he left Wigram for England, he had 157 hours in his logbook, 93 of them solo. With regard to ground training, the official report on L.A.C. Checketts considered that he showed 'commendable keenness throughout his training', with armament his best subject. As for flying ability, he was thought 'A good average pilot who handles his aeroplane smoothly. He has dash but must guard against becoming over confident.' In general, he was thought 'intelligent, hard-working and keen. . . reliable and of good appearance and of a cheerful disposition. In his efforts to learn and acquaint himself with all points relating to his flying he has been outstanding.' He finally qualified as a service pilot on 14 June 1941 and, to his astonishment, was commissioned. Although still average as pilot, navigator and gunner, he was rated 'above average' as a bomb aimer.

The new pilot officer spent some of his embarkation leave at home with his father and sister, some in Christchurch with Natalie. These were tense days for both of them, which they filled as best they could — talking, walking and going to the pictures — but knowing that they would soon be far apart. In fact, when they said their last farewells at Christchurch railway station, more than four years would pass before they met again.

Johnny sailed from Auckland on 22 July 1941 in *The Dominion Monarch* with a cheerful company, mostly of airmen going to train in Canada; many were years younger than Johnny, but few could match his experience in the air. This knowledge was good for his morale, once he had overcome the pang of leaving home for an unknown — though certainly dangerous — future. His chances of returning safely were, in fact, no better than three to one. 10,950

New Zealanders served with the Royal Air Force in World War II of whom 3,285 were killed; 548 became Prisoners of War and many others were wounded. These odds, even if he had known them, would not have discouraged him. He was at last embarked upon what he knew to be the great adventure of his life and was determined to enjoy every moment he could. When the voyage got properly under way, his spirits quickly rose to their usual high level. Sailing through the Panama Canal and calling at Curaçao, he was as content with life as the most carefree tourist of happier days. In the Atlantic, however, heavy grey seas and fear of U-boats together dampened his spirits again. The ship spent a fortnight in Halifax, Nova Scotia, and he was able to go ashore every day. There he saw his first Hawker Hurricane fighter and even managed to sit in the cockpit for a thrilling and apprehensive moment: 'I'd never seen anything like it,' he remembered, 'knobs and dials everywhere, but I knew I could master them. The Hurricane seemed so big and powerful, I just wished I could have learned to fly her there and then.' A few days later, he caught a glimpse of Ireland and was quite overcome because that was the land from which 'my little grandmother had left to sail to New Zealand so many years before'.

As he sailed up the Mersey towards the port of Liverpool, he saw his first signs of war — the twisted superstructures of ships mined and bombed by the Germans — and had his last taste of New Zealand beer. The ship anchored in the stream and Mr W. J. Jordan, the New Zealand High Commissioner, came aboard to speak to the assembled airmen. 'Uncle Bill', who already enjoyed a high reputation in British governing circles, became known to thousands of New Zealanders during the war and was greatly admired for his friendly manner and readiness to look into genuine grievances or problems. Soon after the war ended, he would be an honoured guest at Johnny's wedding. The airmen disembarked straight into a train and as they travelled slowly away from Liverpool, Johnny stared out of the window at wrecked houses and factories, acutely aware that he had, at last, joined the war.

He and the other pilots eventually reached a reception centre at the other end of England, Bournemouth on the south coast, where they stayed about a fortnight. There they were billetted in empty houses, sleeping rough on straw mattresses and provided with but a single blanket. During that time, he was able to visit London. After losing himself in the Underground for about an hour, he managed to reach his objective, the statue of Eros in Piccadilly, only to find that it had been taken away 'for the duration'. While standing there and thinking elevated thoughts — that no member of his family had visited Britain for almost a century and yet he had returned to help Britain resist an aggressive tyranny — he received the first proposition of his sheltered life. A young woman came up to him, smiling: 'Do you want a naughty girl for the afternoon?' Such things were not said in Invercargill and Johnny took to his heels, too embarrassed even to reply.

On returning to Bournemouth, he was delighted to learn that he (and four other New Zealanders) had been posted to No. 56 Operational Training Unit at Sutton Bridge in Lincolnshire, near The Wash, with effect from 16 September 1941. He would be taught to fly the Hurricane and, if he proved good enough, might become a fighter pilot. He came under the command of Flight Lieutenant C. O. J. Pegge, a charming man who had fought in the Battle of Britain. Sutton Bridge had been a Fighter Command armament practice camp before the war and was a grimly utilitarian place. The rooms were small, dark and cold, and half a bucketful of coal had to last twenty-four hours. To a man fresh from New Zealand, the food seemed poor in quality and barely adequate in quantity. Johnny would be posted three times to Sutton Bridge during the war. It never looked any better or felt much warmer, even in summer. But as he got to know the people and the wildlife, he grew to love the area. After Biggin Hill, it became his favourite place in England. The war came close to Sutton Bridge because German E-boats would sometimes hide in The Wash during the night, waiting to pounce on east coast convoys with torpedoes and guns and then race home across the North Sea.

At first, Johnny had little to do. He was not permitted to fly because he had no experience of monoplanes. From time to time, however, he was taken up in various aircraft: a de Havilland Rapide, a Miles Master and the inevitable Tiger Moth. Johnny loved his early flights, even as a passenger. The Wash and The Fens further south were so beautiful and the sky full of aircraft which he had hitherto known only from pictures: Hampdens, Wellingtons, Whitleys, Beauforts, Blenheims and many others. Nevertheless, he was anxious about his future because he had heard that the chief flying instructor wanted to send him and the other New Zealanders to a less advanced training school. To his relief, Joe Pegge announced that work on the Master would begin on 28 September. The Master was an advanced trainer, the first monoplane he ever flew; in comparison to the biplanes on which he learned to fly, it seemed to him alarmingly modern and fast. Pilots were required to prove they could handle the Master solo before they were allowed to tackle the Hurricane. In looks, if not in performance, it was 'almost a facsimile' of the Hurricane, wrote Duncan Smith, 'a splendid transitional aeroplane for the more serious business of flying single-seater fighters'. On his second day in the Master, Johnny successfully got through his first solo.

On 4 October 1941 he had his first flight in a Hurricane. 'The pilot must concentrate all the time,' wrote René Mouchotte (a great French fighter pilot with whom Johnny would serve at Biggin Hill in 1943) when he was first introduced to that aircraft, 'in this little factory transformed into a meteor he is at once radio operator, navigator, engineer and fighter. He subjects himself to terrifying acceleration, tremendous pressure, enormous differences in altitude, in a few minutes. Alone in his plane, he puts his nerves to a grim test. His health must be perfect. So, a fortnight ago, I decided not to smoke any more.' This was one resolution which René did not keep and one which Johnny never made; smoking did not prevent either man from earning distinction in the air.

With a total of 203 hours experience in the air (137 solo, of which 25 were in the Hurricane), he was posted to his first operational squadron early in November. His Natural Aptitude for flying was rated Above Average; in Persistence, Sense of Responsibility, Endurance, Leadership, Initiative, Dash and Self-Control he was also thought Above Average. In Method, Deliberation and Distribution of Attention, however, he was only Average. Overall, he was assessed as 'A keen above the average pilot [who] has worked very hard and progressed greatly. His ground and air discipline are good.' As he himself has said — both ruefully and proudly — 'It was all a far cry from Taieri!'

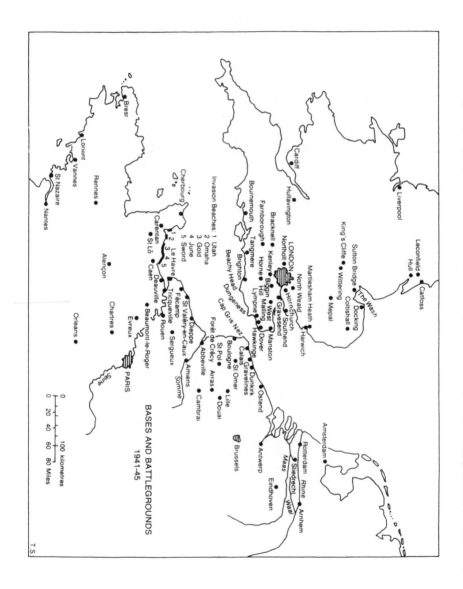

BASES AND BATTLEGROUNDS
1941-45

Invasion Beaches: 1 Utah
2 Omaha
3 Gold
4 June
5 Sword

0   20   40   60   80 Miles
0      40      100 kilometres

T.S.

CHAPTER FOUR

# Learning to Fight: November 1941 to May 1942

Having been taught to fly the Hurricane, Johnny was astonished early in November to find himself in a Spitfire squadron. This was 485 Squadron, the first in Fighter Command to be identified with New Zealand. Formed in March 1941, it was then based at Kenley, south of London in east Surrey, one of the most famous aerodromes in Fighter Command. The standard of comfort was far superior to that available at Sutton Bridge and he was delighted with his good fortune. But Squadron Leader Marcus Knight, a New Zealander who had joined the Royal Air Force in 1935, did not even speak to him after the day he arrived and Johnny was therefore pleased when Knight left the squadron before the end of the month. He was replaced by the senior flight commander, a man of altogether different stamp: Edward Preston Wells (usually known as Bill) had earned the nickname Hawkeye during the Battle of Britain for his exceptional vision and ended the war widely regarded as one of New Zealand's greatest fighter pilots.

Doug Brown, joining the squadron on 8 December as a sergeant pilot, recalled (in a letter home) how the new C.O. came up to him and said: 'I'm Bill Wells, who are you? Have a beer.' Doug, like Johnny, loved Kenley: 'The billets are great,' he wrote, 'with cupboards'. There were good fires and plenty of food 'served and

37

cooked by WAAFs, who are a jolly sight better than men.' The pilots, he thought, were a 'great mob of chaps, no baloney, do anything for you, eager to fight and never let you down — there is no distinction between sergeants and officers, they are all Bill, Tom, Dick, etc. . . . we are flying the fastest type of Spit and they are a fine job. As regards walking, that is over, you pick up the 'phone and ask for the van, and over it comes driven by Waffles — a WAAF,' Apart from one Canadian (Wally McLeod, who became an outstanding fighter pilot in Malta and Normandy) and one Englishman, all the pilots were New Zealanders. Most of the ground crews and administration staffs, however, were British. Once they realised it was not a pose, they relished the New Zealanders' strong aversion to rank or class barriers and this greatly helped to weld the squadron into a family unit. At that time, 485 Squadron had recently been re-equipped with the latest Spitfire, the Mark Vb model, armed with two 20mm Hispano cannon and four .303 inch Browning machine-guns. Together with two other squadrons, No. 452 (Australian) and No. 602 (City of Glasgow), it formed the Kenley Wing under a famous Battle of Britain pilot, John Peel.

An even more famous pilot, Alan Deere, commanded 602 Squadron. Alan's amazing achievements in that battle — of sheer survival, quite apart from victories in aerial combat — had already made him well known to Johnny and nothing in his war experiences gives him more lasting satisfaction than the knowledge that he and Alan became, and have remained, firm friends. Both men have Irish blood and the blarney that goes with it, both are South Islanders (Alan from Westport, on the west coast) and both were brought up in sparsely populated parts of New Zealand where, as Alan wrote, character is 'moulded and toughened in a pioneering atmosphere of independence and adventure'. Alan, having the necessary educational qualifications as well as the necessary enthusiasm and ability, had joined the Royal Air Force in 1937 at the age of nineteen and had earned a reputation in rugby and boxing circles before the war.

He clearly remembered his first meeting with Johnny on 7 November 1941. 'I noticed a dejected-looking Pilot Officer,' he wrote, 'sitting alone in the anteroom and looking as if he would rather be elsewhere. He looked a little older than the average run of officers of his rank and I assumed that he was a newly-commissioned NCO pilot . . . I decided therefore to have a word with him. "What's your name?" I asked, walking over to where he sat. "Checketts, Sir," he answered, leaping to his feet. "Why so depressed, don't you like it here?" "Oh yes. But I was trained on Hurricanes, and Spitfires are new to me. I did my first trip this afternoon and couldn't get the approach right, my speed was always too high. In the end, Bill Crawford-Compton took off and led me in to land. Now I'm afraid the squadron commander might get rid of me." "Of course he won't. Even experienced Spitfire pilots overshoot this airfield. What did Bill say?" "He was very nice and just said that I wasn't to worry about it." Alan took him for a drink and Johnny was soon put at his ease. 'As a result of this incident,' Deere recalled, 'I took a personal interest in Johnny Checketts' career, and was pleased to see that he soon made his mark in the squadron.' Bill Crawford-Compton (who ended his career as an Air Vice-Marshal) was a fellow Southlander, born in Invercargill. The friendship of Alan, Bill and Johnny, forged at Kenley, would outlast the war.

Wherever he turned, Johnny found himself in the presence of men whose reputations within the service were already high. The station commander, for example, was Group Captain (later Air Marshal Sir Cecil) Bouchier. Daddy Bouchier, as he was known to Johnny (he had been Boy Bouchier in World War I), was liked and respected by most pilots. He seemed greatly taken with Johnny's skill at rolling his own cigarettes, using loose tobacco and tissue papers sent to him by his father, and insisted on instruction in the art. For a few blessed minutes the war was put out of mind while they shared some simple fun, surrounded by a chorus of New Zealanders commenting tartly on the performance of both the instructor and his pupil. Like all good commanders, Johnny reflected, Bouchier knew when to fool about and when to crack the whip. Consequently, Kenley was a happy station where 'we worked hard, but didn't feel we had to march about at attention with long faces all the time'.

Fighter Command and No. 2 Group Bomber Command were then undertaking daylight offensive operations. There were four types of escort directly concerned with bomber protection: *close escort* around the bombers; *escort cover* to protect the close escort fighters; *high cover* to prevent enemy fighters taking up position above these formations; and *top cover* to sweep the skies clear of enemy fighters threatening the immediate area of the bombers' target. In these escorts, the fighters naturally adhered closely to bomber courses and timings to and from the target. Other escorts, however, were of a more indirect kind and intended primarily to shoot down enemy fighters enticed into the air by the bombers. Supporting fighter sweeps, routed into an entirely different area, were employed when the penetration of the raid was sufficiently deep to cause the Germans to send reinforcement fighters from bases not immediately threatened. Tactics were a matter for the wing leader concerned, but it was usual for a wing employed on close escort to split: one squadron (twelve aircraft in three sections) would position a section on either side of the bombers with a third slightly above and behind; the other two squadrons would fly above and behind this formation.

This pattern, wrote Deere, 'was a direct copy of that used by the Luftwaffe in the Battle of Britain', but the German aim had then been to destroy Fighter Command 'primarily by bombing, with aerial combat a necessary adjunct'. In 1941, by contrast, the Royal Air Force's aim 'was to entice the Luftwaffe fighters into the air with the object of destroying as many of them as possible . . . In effect, the bombers were the bait; they were inadequate, both in numbers and in weight of bombs carried, to threaten seriously worthwhile enemy targets.' They should have been provided with the minimum escort necessary to permit them to carry out their raids while the rest of the available fighters roamed freely throughout the battle area. Close escort was the most hazardous of the escort tasks, hated and feared by those detailed to carry it out. On the other hand, the squadrons were so well manned by late 1941 that no pilot was required for every mission. There was ample time for training, in the absence of German raids on England, and Johnny was therefore able to learn to handle the Spitfire properly before being called upon to use it as a weapon. His first flight was on 7 November and during the rest of that month, despite very poor weather, he managed to spend some fourteen hours in the air, practising formation flying, dog fighting and cine-camera shooting. Bill Crawford-Compton gave him much sensible advice on the Spitfire's characteristics and he soon fell in love with that beautiful machine: it seemed so light and agile after the Hurricane, though not so easy to land safely. But it was 'a small target', as Doug Brown reminded his family in a letter home, 'so keep hoping'.

Once Hawkeye Wells had succeeded Marcus Knight in command of 485 Squadron, Johnny began to feel very much more at home, surrounded as he was by so many fellow countrymen — even if most of them were from the North Island. Nevertheless, he and Wally McLeod, the solitary Canadian pilot, became good friends until Wally was posted to a Canadian squadron and Johnny missed his cheerful company. Several pilots arrived before Christmas and he no longer felt quite such a new boy. Moreover, having trained on Hurricanes before turning to Spitfires, he believed that he had an advantage over most of his comrades. He was then nearly thirty; years older than all his fellow pilots and unusually old to begin an operational career, but he soon showed himself to be an excellent shot — on the ground, if not yet in the air. Given the high speeds of fighter aircraft, moving at over 150 metres per second, there was hardly any time to adjust aim during combat. The pilot's reflector sight enabled him to know his *range,* but he still had to judge how much deflection — or lead — was necessary to hit a moving target. 'The average standard of shooting in Fighter Command was not high,' wrote Johnnie Johnson, 'for too little attention had been devoted to gunnery instruction.' Most pilots 'hose-piped their machine guns from skidding aeroplanes, opened fire from absurd ranges, and could not estimate their amount of forward allowance.'

The squadron had been provided with clay bird traps and two shotguns to help pilots improve their deflection shooting. Little had been done to set up a proper shooting range, however, until Johnny arrived. He quickly convinced everyone that this was an exciting sport as well as a necessary chore and Hawkeye Wells — a New Zealand champion at clay bird shooting — gave his wholehearted support. Hawkeye, a confirmed gambler, would bet on anything. He proposed a competition: all pilots to enter and put two shillings and sixpence each into the kitty; they would shoot in turn and one miss meant elimination. Soon only Hawkeye, Johnny and Ross Falls survived. Johnny then missed, leaving Hawkeye and Ross to contest a Grand Final worth about four pounds. To general astonishment, Ross won. 'Congratulations,' said Hawkeye, 'shall we try again, double or quits?' Ross unwisely agreed and Hawkeye promptly defeated him, gleefully collecting eight pounds — a handsome sum in those days. Although Johnny was certain that Hawkeye planned this result, he would never admit it, but at least all the competitors helped their new Commanding Officer to drink his winnings. And thereafter some of the wiser pilots practised regularly on Johnny's range.

Whenever the weather relented in that hard winter, Johnny practised flying solo and in formation. At Christmas, his first away from home, he missed Natalie and his family acutely — the more so since Japan was now in the war and the danger to New Zealand seemed very real. He was also anxious about his own future: the longer his first contact with the Luftwaffe was delayed, the more he wondered how well he would meet that challenge. Letters and food parcels from home greatly eased the strain, even though Alan Deere competed vigorously with him for the New Zealand Number Ten pipe tobacco which they both preferred.

On New Year's Eve, Johnny went into London, armed with a forty-eight-hour pass, to see the sights and met Alan quite by chance coming out of the Strand Palace Hotel. He was with his fiancée Joan, who had travelled from Birmingham that morning to have lunch with him. Having taken Joan to the railway station, Alan proposed that he and Johnny go to the Sussex, 'a death trap,' he recalled, 'once you got in, it was difficult to get out sober because practically everyone you knew was also there.' Johnny, who still wanted to see the sights, protested, but Alan said they wouldn't stay long: 'We'll have a salmon sandwich, a pint of beer, and leave.' As it happened, they left when it closed, 'very full of fluid'. An Australian pilot, Eric Evans (with whom Johnny had become friends on the voyage to England), invited them back to his room at the Regent Palace Hotel, where he produced a remarkable number of beer bottles from under his bed. At 11.15 p.m. Alan announced that he must see the new year in at Bobby Page's. Bobby was a wholesale florist merchant in Covent Garden. His warehouse was at street level and below it lay his Kimul Club, a place where Johnny would spend many happy hours during the next four years. Bobby had served in the Royal Flying Corps during World War I and airmen were therefore always welcome in his club. He was also a great friend of actors and actresses who used the club as a rendezvous.

As Alan and Johnny hurried through Leicester Square, Alan accidentally bumped into a group of three soldiers staggering uncertainly in the opposite direction. The soldiers offered to fight Alan, which proved a mistake not only because he was obviously holding his beer much better than they were but because he was at that time the Royal Air Force's reigning middleweight boxing champion. 'I didn't even have time to hold his coat,' said Johnny. 'He knocked the first fellow out very quickly; gave the fellow who attacked him next an awful bump and sat him on the footpath, and the third fellow backed off.' Opposite the Odeon cinema they found a taxi. An army officer wearing a splendid uniform — Johnny remembers blue trousers with a broad scarlet stripe — was climbing in, leaving an elegant lady standing on the pavement. The officer suddenly popped backwards out of the taxi and sat down, much to the astonishment of the elegant lady, Johnny and, no doubt, himself. Alan, having entered the taxi from the road side, had simply pushed the unsuspecting officer out. He then grabbed Johnny and together they were whisked off to Bobby's club in Covent Garden, just in time to welcome 1942. It is only fair to add that Alan's memory of these incidents is less dramatic than Johnny's, but what really matters is that the evening established their friendship.

At the Kimul Club, Johnny met the redoubtable Adolph Gysbert Malan, always known as Sailor in memory of his nine years as a merchant seaman before joining the Royal Air Force. After Alan Deere, Sailor Malan would have the greatest influence on Johnny's fighting career. Sailor had joined the Royal Navy Reserve when war threatened, but found that Regular officers regarded Reservists as a low form of life. 'The difference in relations when I joined the RAF was remarkable,' he wrote later. 'I dare say that as a man from the Dominions I was to some extent favoured. The RAF liked chaps from the Empire.' This feeling of being wanted (as opposed to needed) must have played some part in the determination of Malan, Deere, Checketts and so many other imperial sons to justify their welcome.

Alan had to return to Kenley on New Year's Day and Johnny was again on his own. He met Eric Stewart, a pilot in Coastal

Command, who came from Winton, near Invercargill. They had a happy day together, rounded off with a visit to the Windmill Theatre, where they were both entranced by the sight of so many girls wearing so little. Unfortunately, they had dined too well and, consequently, made so much noise that they were politely invited to leave. They bade each other a cheerful farewell, promising to get together again soon. Johnny caught the train for Kenley; Eric returned to his unit and was killed two weeks later.

Even though Johnny had not yet flown operationally, he began to believe himself part of the scene at Kenley in the early days of 1942. He was learning all he could, not least about the vital part played by ground crews, and agreed with René Mouchotte's tribute to them. The pilot, René wrote, 'must wholeheartedly recognise the devotion of these good lads. In all kinds of weather, rain, frost, at night, they carry on an ungrateful task with no glory attached to it, which every mechanic worthy of the name knows to be necessary and of high value. He, on his side, as a rule appreciates his pilot's merits; he will admire him before all others and his team-spirit will function. I have always regarded these principles as essential during my life as a pilot.'

Johnny at last began to earn his pay on 7 January, taking part in a sweep across the Channel. To his intense annoyance, engine trouble obliged him to return early, but on 12 January he accompanied the wing in a mission covering a commando unit returning from France. As tailend Charlie in a section of four Spitfires flying line astern, he soon found himself exhausted by the effort needed to keep in touch with the other Spitfires while weaving constantly to protect their tails; his fuel was also used up more rapidly, leaving him in greater danger on the return journey of having to bale out over the Channel. Although he quickly came to believe that the line astern formation left the last man unnecessarily vulnerable, that formation was then common throughout Fighter Command and Johnny was too junior even to contemplate changing it.

On 25 January 1942 Group Captain Victor Beamish replaced Bouchier as station commander at Kenley. Beamish was a Southern Irishman with a great reputation within the service and Johnny soon realised why: 'He'd do anything to help you, whatever your job — pilot or ground crew, clerk or cook — as long as you were doing your best, but he was very rough on slackers.' Bill Crawford-Compton replaced Harold Strang (killed on 26 January) as B Flight Commander and gave Johnny much good advice on aerial fighting, but Alan Deere remained his principal tutor until his departure for the United States at the end of January to visit fighter stations and discuss with American pilots the facts of life in aerial combat. Johnny questioned him at great length and took very much to heart his golden rule: always turn towards the attack, never turn away. That rule saved his life many times.

When the weather was doubtful — too bad for planned operations but just good enough for flying — raids known as Rhubarbs were made. A pair of fighters flew at low level over Occupied Europe seeking so-called 'targets of opportunity'. If they ran into a flock of German fighters or found ground fire too fierce, it was supposed that they could make their escape with the help of convenient clouds. Johnny took part in a few Rhubarbs because he loved flying and wanted all the experience he could get, but he soon realised that there was little point in them: bored or angry pilots certainly let off some steam, but only rarely did they strike a useful blow and too many casualties were suffered both by airmen and civilians in France, Belgium or Holland. He agreed with Alan Deere, who wrote that he could not truthfully say that the vehicles and a train which he attacked were strictly military targets. Rhubarbs, significantly, were always voluntary and many pilots refused to consider them.

'If you want to remember the low point of the war,' wrote J. B. Priestley in 1945, 'turn back to the early weeks of 1942, when everything seemed to be going wrong everywhere: Rommel advancing in Libya; German battleships escaping up the Channel; Singapore falling with mysterious ease; the Japs swarming over the Far East like yellow fever. . .' The German ships he had in mind were the battle cruisers *Scharnhorst* and *Gneisenau* and the heavy cruiser *Prinz Eugen* which broke out of Brest on the evening of 11 February, dashed up the Channel during the following day (escorted by destroyers and E-boats, covered by numerous fighters) and reached the sanctuary of home waters.

The weather was very poor on the day of the Channel Dash and at Kenley all hands, including pilots, were out sweeping snow off the runways in order to permit reconnaissance flights to take place. The whole wing was ordered to escort Bristol Beaufort torpedo-bombers in an attack on the German fleet early in the afternoon, Johnny flying as tailend Charlie in Hawkeye Wells's section of four fighters. Although the Beauforts were not found, the wing swept north, despite a low cloud base, snow, sleet and rain, and made contact with the fleet off Ostend. It was ploughing through heavy seas at high speed and the smaller vessels — destroyers and E-boats — were engulfed in green water most of the time. The section led by Wells encountered no enemy fighters, but with fuel running low he decided to tackle an E-boat, a target which four Spitfires might reasonably hope to damage. A fearful wall of anti-aircraft fire was thrown up and Johnny thought it amazing that the Spitfires were not all destroyed. His Spitfire had an old type of canopy with a knockout panel on the port side, so designed that the pilot could dislodge it with his elbow and thus equalise the pressure inside the cockpit with the outside air, should he wish to bale out in a hurry. As Johnny approached the fleet, this panel suddenly flew out of its own volition with a loud bang and for one appalling moment he believed he had been hit. He then realised what had happened and gratefully completed the mission, despite a freezing cockpit, before returning home. The other two sections of 485 Squadron engaged German fighters, claiming four destroyed and several damaged.

That night, writing home to his father, he said: 'I had some luck today and certainly did damage worth a lot of money to the Hun . . . My leader "Hawkeye" took us down on a German escort vessel, an E-boat, and we shot it up good and plenty. We were too busy running from A.A. fire to see what really happened to it so we claimed it as damaged though there was no return fire from it after I fired my burst. I think "Hawkeye" did the most damage and probably killed most of her crew. Anyway, those are my first Huns in return for some close Invercargill friends who have given their lives in the service of the RAF.' Next day, the squadron was much praised in the newspapers for achieving the biggest bag of aerial victories 'and we were interviewed by reporters, much to our dismay', as he told his father. 'Our pictures appeared in the London papers and we feel very small in consequence. Probably you will have read in the papers of these doings because they were certainly historic. Wonderful acts of bravery on the part of certain airmen, who gave their lives, were really worthy of the highest honours this country can bestow.' He had especially in mind Lieutenant Commander Eugene Esmonde, posthumously awarded the Victoria Cross for leading six Fairey Swordfish torpedo-bombers, all destroyed in a virtually unescorted attack upon the fleet.

The squadron was very jubilant at having raised its claim for German aircraft destroyed to twenty, and on 14 February a photograph of its pilots appeared on the front page of the *Daily Express* under a banner headline: 'Whatever Questions May Be Asked [about the conduct of the naval and air forces specially charged to prevent a successful Channel Dash], These Men Did A Grand Job For Britain.' This was the first time he had been mentioned in the newspapers, as Natalie Grover proudly record-ed in her scrapbook. 'NZ Airmen Did Grand Job For Britain' was the bold headline in the Christchurch *Press* on 18 February, followed by a long account of the action: 'Pilot Officer J. M. Checketts, of Invercargill' was one of those who 'pumped an E-boat full of cannon shells and bullets.' An Invercargill newspaper, the *Southland Times,* now singled him out. 'He is well known in sporting circles in the city,' it reported on 19 February (the day before his 30th birthday), 'particularly as one of the most suc-cessful racing motor-cyclists in the province. He enjoyed a brilliant series of successes at broadsiding meetings and hill climbing events a few years ago and was one of the most consistent winners of the silver sash, the premier trophy in the sport. He was also prom-inent among duck and snipe shooters before he joined the Air Force and was an enthusiastic golfer, rower and badminton player.'

Though embarrassed by the publicity, Johnny was relieved to find that he could play his part in operations; he was no more frightened than anyone else and was beginning to see how he could make himself useful. He learned all that he could about the characteristics of machine-guns and cannons and continued to work hard at the problems of deflection shooting, because over Northern France and the Low Countries, where the Luftwaffe fought at times and places of its own choosing, good deflection shooting, as Alan Deere has written, was a must. Johnny also tried to describe to his sister in New Zealand what it was like to fly fighters. 'It is a bit cold here,' he told her, 'I was up at 30,000 feet and it was so cold my breath condensed in my oxygen mask and froze into drops of ice. I coughed and nearly choked myself with the ice I broke off and swallowed. There was ice inside my windscreen so thick that I had to stooge about and scratch it off with my finger nails before I could land. The condensed exhaust gases left behind a thick white trail and as we descended I could see every turn and manoeuvre we had made. This is a remarkable sight. These trails can be seen from the ground and the aircraft can neither be seen nor heard. They are pure white like clouds and stay there for some time. They are really pretty and are only made when the 'planes are very high.'

Off duty, although he had some happy times in the Tudor Rose at Old Coulsdon and in the pubs of Caterham, he was glad to find a more positive form of relaxation. Through Tony Robson (a 485 Squadron pilot) he began a life-long friendship with John Ferguson, a New Zealander affectionately remembered by everyone who served in that squadron. Fergie (as he was usually known) had been wounded at Ypres in 1917. After the war he married his nurse and settled at Oxted, a village about twelve kilometres south of Kenley. Fergie and his wife 'adopted' the squadron and kept open house for airmen of all ranks; as many as four or five could be found staying there at any one time. They repaid his hospitality by helping him with his small electrical goods business. Johnny loved to spend his spare time with Fergie, fitting new elements into electric irons and kettles, and getting to know the local people. The business prospered after the war (Winston Churchill, no less, was among the regular customers) and the Fergusons paid several visits to New Zealand to keep in touch with their 'boys', among whom Johnny was always a special favourite. Johnny also loved golf and sometimes played at Kenley with Pam Barton, then a WAAF officer but formerly a champion golfer. She was so keen to learn to fly that she willingly darned socks and sewed on buttons in return for tuition in the squadron's Magister. Later she would lose her life in an aircraft accident, burnt to death in a Tiger Moth.

At the end of February, Victor Beamish called all the Australian and New Zealand airmen at Kenley to a meeting. The Air Ministry, he said, had instructed him to tell them that they could return home, if they wished. The Japanese, then running riot everywhere in South-east Asia, posed a real danger to Australia and New Zealand. 'I don't know what you could do if you did get home,' said Beamish, 'and I certainly don't want to lose you, but it's up to you. If you wish, you can leave tomorrow.' No-one chose to leave. Everyone recognised, thought Johnny, that the main battle would be fought in Europe; everyone also recognised that there was precious little to fight with in Australia or New Zealand at that time.

He had his first contact with enemy aircraft on 14 March 1942, when the squadron flew to Le Havre as close escort to some Douglas Boston bombers. He was still a tailend Charlie, weaving away to little purpose on the starboard edge of the squadron. En route, an E-boat was spotted and everyone dived to attack it. While they were climbing back into position above the Bostons, Johnny saw a pair of Me 109s following the Spitfires. He gave his warning calmly while the leading German pilot, no less calmly, singled him out and attacked, hitting the Spitfire forward of the cockpit. Johnny turned into the attack, screaming for help. None came. His leader flew on, followed by everyone else. Johnny was spared the fate of so many tailend Charlies partly by his instinctive turn towards the German and partly by a simple mistake. He tried to lower his seat, to get as much of his body behind the armour-plated back as possible, but in his haste he pulled the firing mechanism for the Plessey gun, loaded with Very cartridges displaying particular colours as identification signals. He heard three loud bangs, the cockpit filled with cordite fumes and he thought his last moments had come. Nothing worse happened, however, and he soon realised that his enemy had dived away — unnerved, perhaps, by the flares shooting out of the Spitfire. The incident taught Johnny a vital lesson: 'There are very few men you can count on in a crisis; as a rule, you have to look out for yourself — first, last and always.'

Brendan 'Paddy' Finucane, a flight commander in 452 (Australian) Squadron, had succeeded Alan Deere in command of 602 Squadron. Like Beamish, who promoted him, Paddy was a Southern Irishman and Johnny already admired him for his magnificent combat record and very strong personality: He had the rare gift of command without being at all bossy. There was, however, some suspicion at Kenley and, indeed, throughout 11

Group regarding the Australian squadron's high victory claims. These victories naturally attracted intense press publicity which, in turn, added jealousy to the suspicion. Both centred around Finucane and, thought Johnny, unsettled him. Johnny himself was sometimes surprised at the number of successes enjoyed by the Australians on occasions when it seemed to him that few German fighters were about. But what annoyed him far more was their complete lack of radio discipline in the air: 'They were such noisy beggars, continually yelling and screaming at each other — and everybody else, for that matter. It made fighting quite difficult because no orders could be transmitted by other units while the air was filled with such a ceaseless racket.' Finucane would lead 602 Squadron with great distinction until June 1942, when he was promoted to wing commander and sent to lead the Hornchurch Wing. Sadly, he lost his life in July and Johnny still remembers the widespread grief felt at Kenley when the news became known.

Johnny continued to fly as a tailend Charlie and continued to feel unnecessarily vulnerable. He kept his feelings to himself, however, for junior officers were not encouraged to express opinions on fighting formations. Early in April he was attacked by a Focke-Wulf 190 and hit three times, but thanks to the wise advice of Deere, Wells and Crawford-Compton (and to his own increasing skill) he managed to escape. The Fw 190, aptly named Butcher Bird by the Germans, and 'perhaps the most perfect radial-engined fighter ever built', in the opinion of an authoritative history of German aircraft, 'was certainly the most advanced fighter in the world' when it appeared on the Western Front in September 1941 (though not in substantial numbers before February 1942). 'For the first time the Luftwaffe fighter pilots were to have an ascendancy over the contemporary Spitfire, an ascendancy which they enjoyed at least until the introduction of the Spitfire IX during the autumn of 1942.'

Between March and June that year, Fighter Command and 2 Group lost 314 aircraft in exchange for 90 German aircraft destroyed. Shortly after Johnny's narrow escape from this formidable fighter, Alan Deere (now back in England from the United States) met Hawkeye Wells in the Kimul Club and heard his views on it. The Fw 190, he said, had made a tremendous difference to most German pilots. They were far more aggressive. 'We no longer ask how many we've downed, but how many we've lost. Frankly, it's bloody tough going over the other side now, and I always breathe a sigh of relief when I cross the English coast on the return journey. I bet I'm not the only one, either.'

Bill Crawford-Compton broke his arm during April, leaving Reg Grant — the other flight commander — in line to succeed Hawkeye Wells as squadron commander. Reg was a seasoned campaigner, tough and resourceful, well-liked by many pilots; Johnny certainly respected him, but they were never to become particular friends. April proved to be a busy month for Johnny, by far the busiest he had yet experienced, spending over forty-eight hours in the air: he had flown only seventy-two hours during the previous five months. There were regular sweeps across the Channel and interceptions of German raiders were attempted over England, but few occasions for combat arose. On 25 April, however, while escorting bombers to attack the famous airfield at Abbeville, Johnny did engage an Fw 190: 'I hit him hard too, but couldn't see whether he crashed or not. I didn't claim him.' During the next few days, the squadron found the Luftwaffe reacting vigorously to its intrusions — both fighter sweeps and as bomber escorts — and several casualties were suffered. 'Our stupid line-astern formations,' in Johnny's opinion, 'gave the Germans an advantage they didn't really deserve.'

On 30 April, the King visited Kenley and spoke to several pilots, among them Johnny who thus met him for the first time and was greatly impressed by his gentle, courteous manner — and by how much he knew about aerial fighting. While the King was in the Operations Room, Tony Robson (whose combat film of the destruction of an Fw 190 earlier that month would become world famous) damaged another German fighter and the King remained at Kenley until Robson landed. He was most interested in his first-hand account of what happened, much to Robson's embarrassment, who realised only then that His Majesty had been listening in the Operations Room to the awful language pilots used in combat.

John Kilian, an instructor at Wigram while Johnny was training there, had now joined 485 Squadron. He was usually quiet (one of the qualities Johnny most valued in those hectic, noisy days), but he had a dry, sharp sense of humour which contrasted nicely with the boisterous fun more usually found off duty. Moreover, he was an excellent pilot and Johnny greatly admired his skilful handling of the Spitfire. Friendships became close much more quickly in wartime than in peacetime, Johnny noticed. Men were so much more constantly in each other's company and lived their lives so much more intensely. They were acutely aware that each day might well be their last; they also knew that posting or promotion — as sudden and unpredictable as death or injury — quickly separated friends. In war as in politics, a week was a long time. So it was with Johnny and John Kilian. No sooner had a pattern of friendship been established than Kilian was posted away; Johnny, too, almost left the squadron. Early in May, to his great relief, he was at last considered sufficiently experienced to be moved forward from the tailend Charlie position. From the viewpoint of his personal safety, he never received a more welcome promotion. It is all the more ironical, therefore, that he should be shot down next day.

CHAPTER FIVE

# Learning to Shoot:
# May to December 1942

Johnny was delighted to learn that Alan Deere had returned to England and would take over 403 (Canadian) Squadron at Southend on 1 May. He had had command of 602 (City of Glasgow) Squadron when Johnny first met him and, by a remarkable coincidence, Johnny's service number happened to be 403602. For no reason that will stand logical analysis, as he readily admits, he decided to regard this coincidence as an excellent omen both for Alan and himself. Since both men not only survive to this day, hale and hearty, and remain the best of friends, he argues (with a smile) that logic cannot compete with his beliefs. When Alan left Kenley, he entrusted to Johnny his scots terrier Stevie (named after a friend killed in the Battle of Britain). Stevie was attacked by lice and Johnny had to take him to a vet who shaved off all his hair and kept him for two days while he treated him with some lotion.'When I picked him up,' wrote Johnny, 'the poor wee fellow looked at me and hung his head. He looked so sad and naked.' But Johnny, a dog-lover, ensured that Stevie got the best of care and attention and he was soon bounding about, happy as ever. Before he could face the Luftwaffe again, Alan needed Stevie and so Johnny hopped into a Spitfire, set Stevie on his knee, and flew him down to Southend.

This happy interlude was followed by one of the most frightening experiences of his career. He took part in a fighter sweep on

4 May which was intercepted by German fighters over the Channel a little north of Boulogne. One pilot was hit immediately and Johnny heard him calling for help before he baled out. Moments later, he spotted a Fw 190 on his own tail and turned swiftly into the attack, firing vigorously, only to be hit hard from behind by another Focke-Wulf. He felt a sharp pain in his leg and the Spitfire fell into a spin. After an agonising struggle, he managed to recover some sort of control and since the German pilot had not followed him down, he was able to take hasty stock of his situation. There was a large hole in the cockpit floor near his feet and part of the starboard wing had been shot away, including the radiator.

Clearly, the Spitfire could not stay in the air much longer and Johnny realised immediately that he had no chance of reaching land, friendly or enemy-held. He was well aware that the Spitfire was a notoriously dangerous aircraft to ditch in the sea at the best of times; with a hole in the cockpit floor it would certainly be a fatal move. No sooner had this thought flashed through his mind than the engine seized and the aircraft spun down again. Somehow, he wrestled it on to an even keel, but the sea was now alarmingly close and he knew that he must get out at once or not at all. He baled out, pulled the rip cord as soon as he cleared the cockpit, swung once, and splashed into the water.

He had no time to release the parachute and it collapsed on top of him. While the silken canopy gradually settled around him, holding him under the water, he struggled desperately to claw his dinghy off the parachute's seat and inflate it. The dinghy bobbed to the surface, pulling him with it. His right arm was almost bound to his side by the parachute cords, but he managed to get his pipe-cleaning knife out of his battledress pocket. Opening it carefully with frozen, shaking fingers, he began to hack and saw at the cords. At last, when he was so cold and exhausted that he could scarcely hold the knife or see what he was doing, the final cord gave way and the parachute sank. The knife slipped out of his fingers and for one dreadful moment he lost his hold on the dinghy, forgetting that it was attached by a strap to his mae west. It bounded away, but he soon grabbed it again. Whenever he tried to scramble into it, however, the dinghy turned over and slapped him under the water. He forced himself to relax for a moment, to gulp some air into his lungs and spit out some of the water, to gather his strength for a major effort. Then, as slowly and calmly as he could, he hauled his body into the dinghy.

Johnny felt blissfully at ease — until he realised that the dinghy was half full of icy water and that he had never been so cold, so frightened or so tired in his life. He baled some of the water out and then, for the first time, looked about him. It was late evening, about 9 p.m., and the light was fading fast. He knew that unless he was rescued before dark he had little prospect of seeing another dawn. Looking towards the French coast, he could just make out what seemed to be a buoy with a mast. The Germans, he knew, had a string of rafts moored off the coast to serve as refuges for their own downed airmen and he prayed fervently that the buoy might indicate one of them. He tried to paddle towards it, but was too weak to make much progress. From time to time, he thought he heard aircraft engines and hoped that plenty of keen eyes — preferably British — were looking for distressed airmen.

About ten minutes later, a Westland Lysander passed nearby, but gave no sign of having seen him. He waved and screamed, staring fixedly at it as if this would help the crew to sense his presence. The Lysander continued to cruise around, in what seemed to him a leisurely, unconcerned manner and he was near to panic when suddenly it swooped right over his head and a smoke float was dropped so accurately that it nearly hit him. He paddled eagerly to where it landed. It smelt awful, but it was warm and so he grabbed it and cuddled it lovingly. Then the mast which he had thought attached to a buoy began to approach and turned out to be part of 'a lovely little vessel', HM Motor Launch No. 139, commanded by a Lieutenant Hodson. The launch pulled up alongside the dinghy, a boarding net was dropped and two seamen dragged him aboard. In his log book, Johnny later composed a succinct summary of this shattering experience: 'Shot down in Channel by Fw 190. In dinghy forty-five minutes.'

He was quite unable to stand and suddenly remembered the pain he had felt in his leg when the German fighter attacked him. It proved to be a shrapnel wound, not serious in itself, but it cost him a lot of blood. He was taken below, stripped and given a beer glass full of rum: it went down so easily that he did not even taste it. A seaman dried him vigorously with a very rough towel, rolled him in a blanket with three hot water bottles and then brought him a cup of cocoa, 'so thick that the spoon almost stood up in it.' The seaman made him drink it and then gave him a slice of brown bread, thickly smeared with Marmite. Johnny soon felt surprisingly well. In part, this was a result of brisk, business-like treatment; in part also, it was a result of the wonderful relief at being rescued when a miserable death had seemed only too likely. The seaman returned with his clothes — shrunken and stained, but dry — and he struggled into them. Lieutenant Hodson then invited him up to the bridge, if he felt strong enough. When he got there, the launch was approaching Dover and they berthed just at midnight.

Johnny thought he had never been so happy. The shock and pain of being shot down, the agony and fear in the water, were nothing compared to the joy of being alive and only slightly injured. The German pilot could so easily have killed him, but at least it would have been quick. Just a sudden thump then nothing; not a bad way to go. This experience played its part in his later success as a fighter pilot. Although he continued to take sensible precautions against being killed, and had his share of fearful moments, never again would he be apprehensive about the prospect of combat in the air. Should some German hit him where it hurt most, that would be a pity, but with luck he would not feel much for long. Unless and until that happened, however, he would keep calm, think before he acted, and do some hitting on his own account.

Meanwhile, a little celebration was in order. he had with him his escape purse, issued to all pilots flying over enemy territory. It had 2,000 French francs in it (worth ten pounds sterling). He gave it to Hodson, who produced a bottle of rum in exchange, and they drank it together. It seemed a good idea at the time, but Johnny felt so ill afterwards that he foreswore rum for ever. Dave Clouston, one of the squadron pilots, arrived next morning in a Miles Magister and took him home to Kenley. The reaction to his brush with death was hitting him by then, as well as the rum, but he felt much worse when he learned that his comrades had already shared out most of his clothes. He got them back, eventually. More happily, he learned that he owed his life to Reg Baker of Dunedin. Reg had seen a parachute open and flop into the sea. He promptly transmitted a distress signal which enabled the air-sea rescue service to fix the spot where a pilot, British or German, was known to have come down. Johnny was already fond of Reg and, not surprisingly, they became great friends, but Reg was killed later in the war. The squadron adjutant wrote to the Irving Parachute Company to inform them that yet another pilot had been saved by their product and thereby qualified for membership of the Caterpillar Club. Irving sent Johnny a golden caterpillar, suitably inscribed. It has red eyes, to signify that his escape was a hot one, from an aircraft on fire. His wife now regards it as one of her most precious possessions and often wears it on special occasions.

Within three days of being pulled out of the Channel, Johnny was crossing it again. On 16 May, he and another pilot carried out a low-level strafing sortie in bad weather over the small port of St. Valery-en-Caux, where the famous 51st (Highland) Division had been forced to surrender to Rommel in June 1940. The two pilots tried to blow up a gas tank there, but it was too close to a cliff and so they had to content themselves with destroying a railway signal box and firing on a locomotive shed and German troops crossing a bridge before escaping untouched, either by ground fire or enemy aircraft. Day after day, he was out on similar missions or large-scale fighter sweeps, on bomber escorts or attempts to intercept German fighters attacking towns on the southeast coast of England. On one of these operations, he encountered a Fw 190 for the first time since he was shot down. Without flinching even for a moment, he turned eagerly towards the German and hit him hard. He saw his cannon shells strike home, but was unable to pursue far and try to finish him off; he therefore made no claim, not even for 'damaged'.

When Victor Beamish was killed on 28 March 1942, his replacement as Station Commander at Kenley had been Group Captain (later Air Marshal Sir Richard) Atcherley. Like Beamish, 'Batchy' was unwilling to accept that he could no longer handle fighter aircraft in combat. On 26 May he was shot down into the Channel: unlike Beamish, he was rescued and returned to the station after three weeks in hospital. Shortly after Johnny heard the news that Batchy had been shot down, he went into the Mess and was amazed to see him sitting there, large as life. It turned out that this was David, his identical twin brother (later an Air Vice-Marshal). Batchy had been badly wounded in the left arm and David, then Commanding Officer at Fairwood Common (near Swansea), felt a sharp pain in his own left arm at precisely the moment — he learned later — that Batchy suffered his wound. Johnny liked Batchy; he was a very warm, enthusiastic man, always cheerful and friendly to ground crews and pilots alike. The war went on more briskly as the weather improved and Johnny was in action most days. During one fighter sweep over Saint-Omer on 30 May he was engaged by a Fw 190: 'He hit me, too; not badly, but enough to frighten me.' Next day, there was a bomber escort to Gravelines, Abbeville and Boulogne that ended disastrously. Two pilots, Garry Barnett and Stanley Browne, were shot down. Both survived and eventually made their way back to England. Johnny engaged a Focke-Wulf and damaged it; as usual, he made no official claim.

During May, Johnny flew nearly forty-six hours and, not surprisingly, had very little time or energy for social activities beyond a few visits to local pubs and keeping up with the Ferguson family at Oxted. At this time, Kenley was guarded by first class soldiers: officers and men of the Brigade of Guards and the Coldstream Guards, who rather awed unmilitary airmen. Johnny, however, greatly admired their smartness and precision. One morning, after a Colour-hoisting parade, he and a young second lieutenant, whom he had hitherto found polite but reserved, managed for once to get into animated conversation when Johnny noticed that he was carrying a walking stick which turned out to be a beautifully-disguised 410 gauge shotgun. Johnny, who loved guns, invited the officer to try it out on the clay bird trap at the squadron dispersal area and there he immediately showed himself to be a superb shot. They became firm friends until that particular battalion was posted away.

His enthusiasm for shooting also kept him on good terms with Hawkeye Wells. One wet afternoon, when flying had been cancelled for the day, Hawkeye invited Johnny to join him and Victor Hall in a 'pheasant feast'. Taking these birds was an illegal pastime, but there were plenty of them about, service rations were generally unappetising and Johnny shared Hawkeye's opinion that with the Luftwaffe to worry about every day, other problems seemed not to matter much. 'Can you pluck birds?' asked Hawkeye. 'Yes,' answered Johnny, 'but why not get the Mess staff to do it?' 'No fear,' came the reply, 'nobody else gets a piece of this treat. You pluck and clean the bird and put the entrails and feathers down the lavatory. We'll do the cooking in my room in a mess tin over the electric heater. You'll have to pinch some margarine, bread, salt and pepper and we can have a splendid feast.' Johnny obligingly did as he was told, handed over the cleaned bird and went off to the lavatory to dispose of the entrails and feathers. The entrails were no problem, but the feathers scattered all over the cubicle and it took him a good half hour to get rid of all the evidence. When he returned to Hawkeye's room, he found that he and Victor had practically finished the feast. Johnny thus learned another valuable lesson the hard way: never again did he hand over a bird ready for the pot until the unwanted portions had been disposed of.

German squadrons remained in the front line much longer than was usual in the Royal Air Force and many of their pilots, consequently, were very experienced in combat and their tactics superior to those employed by most Royal Air Force squadrons. 'They flew a widely-spaced formation which left them pretty free to act as they pleased,' recalled Johnny. 'They were not tied to our dreadful line astern formations and I often wondered whether the top brass insisted on it or whether it simply appealed to a majority of our senior pilots.' Several German fighter pilots became known to him by name, among them Josef Priller and Hermann Graf. Such men rarely engaged in lengthy dog-fights; one fast pass and away, often before their targets realised they were even in danger.

During the first half of June, Johnny flew over France almost every day, but the Germans usually stayed on the ground. He did not blame them: the Spitfire, when used on offensive sweeps, was too lightly armed to do serious damage to ground targets and its range too short either to permit it to penetrate far inland or make more than a brief pass at any target it managed to find. When used as an escort fighter, the Spitfire proved almost as useless: it lacked the range to accompany bombers all the way to most worthwhile targets and the Luftwaffe, naturally, waited for the escorts to turn for home before attacking the bombers. He well understood by now that he was taking part in a fight quite unlike the Battle of Britain. That had been a defensive battle and the

Spitfire was a superb defensive fighter. Taking the fight to the enemy over France was a different matter altogether because the Germans then had the advantage of fighting on their own terms over their own territory and the freezing waters of the Channel were no longer a British but a German ally.

Daylight operations, beginning on a small scale in December 1940, had been greatly intensified after June 1941 to help the Russians by reducing or even reversing the flow of Luftwaffe units to the East. Unfortunately, the efforts of Fighter Command and the light bombers of 2 Group, Bomber Command, failed. Worse still, their exaggerated victory claims encouraged the Air Ministry to press on despite the heavy losses suffered. Nor did matters improve when the offensive was resumed in March 1942 after a break during the winter for rest and reflection. In the next three months, Fighter Command alone lost 259 aircraft in return for the destruction of fifty-eight German fighters — but it claimed 197 certainly destroyed in that time. Whatever the newspapers said and whatever optimistic speeches were made by visiting senior officers, Johnny knew — from the claims made and losses suffered at Kenley — that this battle was not being won.

On 14 June Johnny was promoted to Flying Officer and next day 485 Squadron was sent to Martlesham Heath near Ipswich in Suffolk for a week to practise air firing at a target drogue. It should have been easy meat for an experienced squadron, shooting regularly at all manner of targets, fixed and moving, but it was not. Although Johnny was disappointed with his own performance (he lost points for shooting the drogue off the tow line), he noticed that a surprising number of his comrades achieved even fewer hits. Shortly after this embarrassing experience, he was sent by Reg Grant (who had succeeded Hawkeye as commander of the squadron in May) to a training school at Sutton Bridge where pilots were carefully taught to use their guns accurately; a skill which, ideally, should have been mastered by all fighter pilots before they were posted to operational squadrons. Johnny was glad to go: he and Reg rarely seemed at ease with each other, but — more important — Johnny knew that he was failing to make the best use of the guns he loved and he knew also that Sailor Malan commanded the school. 'The making of Johnny,' wrote Doug Brown, 'was his posting to Gunnery School, where he learned the skills of air-to-air firing and realised his own ability as a good shot which gave him confidence so necessary to succeed in this area.'

Malan had proved himself one of the best aerial shots in the RAF and Johnny was determined to learn all he could from an acknowledged master and from the other nine officers who took part in the course. He revelled in their company. One had served aboard CAM ships (Catapult Aircraft Merchant ships) which accompanied Atlantic convoys. Each CAM ship carried a single Hurricane fighter, launched by rocket-catapult on the approach of an enemy aircraft. When his Hurricane ran out of fuel, the pilot would bale out as close as possible to a friendly ship or make for a friendly airfield, if one was within range. Having himself experienced the pain and fear of parachuting once into the sea, at a time when the alternative was certain death, Johnny greatly admired the calm courage of a man prepared to do this desperate deed willingly time and time again.

Another member of the course was Pat Bell, who had recently been shot down over France, avoided capture, and returned to England. Johnny questioned Bell closely because 'it occurred to me, that with all the flying we were doing over there, it was quite likely that I'd be shot down again and come down on land the next time. I wanted to learn all the tricks I could to help me evade capture.' His forethought and Bell's practical advice would pay handsome dividends about fifteen months later. A third member of the course was a Polish pilot named Horbaczewski, known to everyone as Horace. Horace was an outstanding pilot: 'The rest of us could fly all right,' said Johnny, 'but Horace did better than that; he really handled a Spitfire beautifully.' Pat Bell, Horace and Johnny became firm friends, constantly in each other's company when off duty.

The school was equipped with Spitfire IIs and Wellingtons (used to train air gunners in warding off fighter attacks). A regular exercise was for the fighters to attack the bombers, both sides armed with camera guns. After the exercise, study of the film produced would show which side had the advantage. Horace and Johnny agreed to fight the Wellingtons as a pair, using the same tactics that they had seen employed by their German enemies. The pair, they found, was a deadly formation: the leader could concentrate on his target, knowing that his partner was covering his tail. The officer in charge of the bombers (Wing Commander Lowe, the only air gunner of that rank whom Johnny met during the war) complained that it was no use sending such experts against his boys: they could never shoot any useful film because they were constantly on the receiving end. Sailor Malan was highly amused, but he quietly advised Horace and Johnny to go easy without making it obvious that they were doing so. Bomber gunners, he said, had to be trained as well as fighter pilots and it was no good undermining their confidence. Johnny saw Sailor's point, but he never afterwards watched British bombers heading towards Germany by night or France by day without a sick feeling in the stomach, knowing as he did how easily a well-handled fighter could bring them down.

Johnny enjoyed himself immensely during his month at Sutton Bridge. Intensive flying in the company of a pilot as expert as Horace helped to improve his own airmanship, weapons training was very much to his taste, he loved the immense skies of East Anglia and the peaceful country scenes; not least, the weather was beautiful, day after day. His ability to hit a moving target improved so much that Sailor rated him above the average as an aerial marksman, though only average at air-to-ground firing and below the average at drogue shooting. 'Has been a very keen pupil,' wrote Sailor, 'and has shown every endeavour to get the best results from the Course. He has had consistent bad luck with his drogue shooting which is bound to improve. Has plenty of dash and his Combat shooting was above the average. Will make a good instructor.' These last words greatly alarmed Johnny: 'I didn't want to be any kind of instructor, good or bad; I wanted to get back to fighting and show myself — and others — how much I'd learned at Sutton Bridge.'

During that month, Johnny and Sailor quickly became friends and would often go out into The Wash at night, shooting widgeon. These little water fowl used to fly in darkness from The Wash to feed in the fields of the Fen Country. They were difficult targets, flying fast and low, and choosing good positions to hunt them was not without danger: many water courses were hard to find (or avoid) even in daylight, some of them were ten feet deep and the tides rose quickly and ran strongly. But Johnny and Sailor felt comfortable in each other's company on such expeditions. True countrymen, they ignored the wet and the cold, kept still and quiet when necessary and did not complain when nothing was caught or even seen. Johnny met an eminent local poacher one night in a nearby pub who promised to take him to some special places in return for a box of cartridges. Like pheasant feasting, this was an illegal act, but he gave him a box on his 'here today, gone tomorrow' principle. They went out to The Wash and Johnny, who considered himself a competent hunter, was most impressed by the poacher's craftsmanship: he moved silently, shot accurately and had mastered many bird calls exactly. Johnny would return to that part of England more than once during the next three years and often went shooting with his poacher friend.

After the course was over, Johnny rejoined his squadron. It had moved from Kenley to King's Cliffe, about twenty kilometres west of Peterborough in Northamptonshire, for a break from frontline operations and Reg Grant welcomed him back on 23 July with something less than exuberance. He took part in a few uneventful convoy patrols off the Norfolk coast (working from a forward air-field at Docking, near the east coast of The Wash) and in the squadron's first night patrol on the 28th, hunting German bombers near Norwich. Two nights later, while seeking more bombers over Birmingham, he was fired on four times by the city's anti-aircraft batteries.

Rumours were already circulating that a major landing was being planned on the French coast, a landing that must be covered by as many fighter aircraft as possible. Johnny was very excited at the prospect of taking part in such a vital action, using the skills he had practised so diligently at Sutton Bridge. This, however, was not to be, for he was posted as an instructor to 1488 Fighter Gunnery Flight at Martlesham Health on 11 August and the Dieppe Raid took place on the 19th. Not since the Battle of Britain had there been such intense air fighting as on that day and Johnny was extremely disappointed to miss it. But he had over 220 operational flying hours to his credit, accumulated during the last nine months, and Reg Grant was entitled to consider him in need of a rest. At least he gave him a good reference. Flying Officer Checketts, he wrote, 'has always shown himself reliable and conscientious. I consider him a good leader and fighter pilot.' Although he did not think so at the time, Johnny was lucky to miss the Dieppe

Raid, for it cost the Royal Air Force heavy casualties: 106 fighters (and 67 pilots) in exchange for only 48 German aircraft; over 4,000 soldiers and sailors were lost.

Despite the coolness between himself and his commanding officer, Johnny loved operational flying so much that he regretted leaving the New Zealand squadron and went reluctantly to Martlesham Heath, where squadrons were sent in turn for a week of intensive training in aerial gunnery. Somewhat to his surprise, he found himself enjoying the work. However, it was alarming to learn that several experienced frontline pilots were, in fact, extremely poor shots who knew next to nothing about the capabilities of their weapons and were reluctant to learn more. The majority, fortunately, were only too keen to practise hard and learn what they could and Johnny was just as keen to help them — and himself at the same time. They used the excellent two-seater Miles Master for their work. His job was to instruct pilots in the principles of deflection shooting in order to hit a moving target while firing from a moving platform. Even though he recognised the value of his work and thought he did it well, he remained anxious to return to the frontline. He sounded out several visiting squadron commanders and applied for a posting to Malta, all to no avail. The best he could manage was one or two unofficial operational flights. Wing Commander Richard Deacon-Elliott, responsible for the allocation of gunnery instructors in No. 11 Group, flatly refused to release him. 'Your fighting days,' he said, 'are finished.' 'Well, if that's the case,' Johnny replied, 'I want to go home to New Zealand because I can get up into the islands and fight there.' When 485 Squadron turned up at Martlesham Heath for its week-long course, he felt particularly restless and even resentful, though he did his best to appear cheerful and at ease with his old friends and acquaintances.

Although the hangars were practically roofless and there was little habitable office space (as a result of the Luftwaffe's efforts during the Battle of Britain), Johnny thought Martlesham Heath a delightful place. Apart from his duty flying, he had the pleasure of taking up a Hurricane again and also enjoyed flights in a Supermarine Walrus, a Boulton Paul Defiant and a Westland Lysander. The airfield lay some fifteen kilometres north of the naval port of Harwich. Ships based there used to escort convoys to Russia and he became friendly with the captain of HMS *Eglington*, a destroyer which had endured some grim experiences at the hands of German aircraft, surface raiders and submarines — to say nothing of dreadful weather — en route to Murmansk. Therefore, whenever he was off-duty and the sky clear, Johnny would borrow a Master and take as many naval officers and men as he could for brief flights over the port and the surrounding countryside. It made a refreshing break from routine and the *Eglington*'s captain was most appreciative. Johnny sometimes dined aboard, and wined very well too, but he avoided rum like the plague. A favourite haunt was the White Horse hotel in Ipswich where sorrows were drowned, though not very deeply, given the weakness of wartime beer. One night at Martlesham Heath, standing on the front lawn to watch an air raid on Harwich, he heard a bomb screaming down much too close for comfort. He sprinted for a slit trench and dived in, landing on top of about eight airmen who had run even faster. The bomb exploded nearby with a tremendous noise, destroying some trees and a building. The trench shook, everyone was spattered with earth and very frightened: 'but we all pretended it was a great joke — afterwards.'

At the end of December, Johnny received a most welcome Christmas present. He learned that he was to return in January 1943 to an operational squadron: 611 (West Lancashire) Squadron, at Biggin Hill, the most famous of all RAF stations. Squadron Leader Hugo Armstrong, an Australian, would be his commanding officer and his friend Sailor Malan had just been appointed station commander. Johnny had already spent a couple of days with that squadron in August, at the invitation of Bill Crawford-Compton, his old 485 Squadron mentor and then a flight commander in 611, but nothing could be done about his posting to Martlesham Heath. Bill did what he could to help Johnny return to operations, though he himself would leave 611 to command 64 Squadron at Hornchurch before Johnny arrived. He greatly admired Bill: 'A very good leader, determined to fight his way to the top — and he did just that.' By the end of 1943, these words applied with equal force to Johnny Checketts.

## CHAPTER SIX

# Fighting: 611 Squadron at Biggin Hill, January to June 1943

The Wing Commander Flying at Biggin Hill was then Dickie Milne, a Battle of Britain pilot whom Johnny had already met at Martlesham Heath. Milne had two squadrons under his command: the Free Frenchmen of 340 (Ile-de-France) Squadron and men from every part of Britain, the Dominions and Occupied Europe in 611 Squadron. Biggin Hill in 1943 had become a veritable United Nations in miniature and Johnny revelled in the happy, purposeful atmosphere of 'the world's premier fighter base', as Wing Commander H. L. Thompson described it, where there was 'an atmosphere of jauntiness and of living with little thought for the morrow'.

There was also more comfort than at most fighter stations. 'Instead of the usual bleak disorder of broken chairs and trellis tables, a wheezy gramophone and ochre walls covered with fly-blown pinups,' recalled Colin Hodgkinson, 'we had [in our crew room] deep sofas and armchairs covered with arty chintz, the latest thing in stoves, and a fine radiogram. A modification to this radiogram linked it up with the Very High Frequency sets in the aircraft, so that whenever the squadron was operating all who were not on the show could lean back comfortably and listen to the dog fight.' Most of the men and women stationed there were certain that they fought, killed or died in a just cause. Consequently, they sensed a bond of fellowship between them that is, perhaps, unique to wartime. 'We lived at last,' wrote J. B. Priestley, 'in a community with a noble common purpose, and the experience was not only novel but exhilarating. We had a glimpse then of what life might be if men and women freely dedicated themselves, not to their appetites and prejudices, their vanities and fears, but to some great communal task.'

Sailor Malan, the newly appointed station commander, welcomed Johnny warmly and was very interested to learn how he had managed to escape from the training world at his relatively advanced age (thirty-one in February) and return to operations. 'By ringing everyone I knew who might even possibly help whenever I could get to a telephone,' replied Johnny. 'I made such a nuisance of myself that they had to move me if only to shut me up.' Sailor smiled; that was the spirit he wanted at Biggin Hill. Morale was exceptionally high there, Johnny thought, and the squadrons very aggressive. And yet, like squadrons elsewhere, they were becoming more cautious — more realistic — in their victory claims. During the first half of 1943, for example, when Fighter Command claimed 249 enemy aircraft destroyed, the actual number was 235. Not since the war began had the gap between desire and fulfilment been so small.

On 13 January 1943 he helped to escort eighteen Ventura bombers in an attack on the airfield at Abbeville. The Luftwaffe reacted forcefully and he soon found himself involved in a furious dogfight with a Fw 190 and only the ability of the Spitfire Vb to turn more tightly than the German fighter saved his life. Nevertheless, he managed to hit it once or twice and eventually it dived away inland; he resisted the temptation to follow. He was now at a low altitude and spotted a column of troops, ammunition waggons and a gun post, all of which he strafed vigorously. He returned home safely and Sailor, having questioned him closely about the dogfight, ordered him to make an official claim for one Fw 190 damaged. Although he believed he had damaged several enemy fighters in 1942, Johnny had never before made an official claim. Suddenly he realised how much he was on probation. Although Sailor regarded him as an agreeable off-duty companion, he had no room at Biggin Hill for pilots who failed to measure up to his high standards. Johnny was untroubled on that score.

He had decided that he was an average man, frightened of being killed; he had also decided that most German pilots were no less average and no less frightened; therefore, if he behaved aggressively in aerial combat, he must have an advantage over most of his opponents. 'I never, ever, avoided a combat,' he wrote, 'and found that this paid because very few Germans cared to fight back if you went for them hard.' As Alfred Price, the distinguished aviation historian put it: 'It isn't the size of the dog in the fight that counts, it's the size of the fight in the dog.'

January proved to be a very busy month: there were fighter sweeps and bomber escorts over France and attempts to intercept German raiders over south-east England on every day when the weather permitted flying. Johnny worked hard to prove his worth in the frontline, but no personal success came his way. Indeed, he needed all his skill and watchfulness simply to stay alive because the Spitfire Vb could not match its German opponents. Casualties mounted steadily and on 5 February Hugo Armstrong, commanding officer of 611 Squadron, was shot down near Cap Gris Nez. Johnny led a squadron for the first time in a hastily-arranged sweep over the area later that day in case Armstrong had baled out and taken to his dinghy, but he was never seen again.

To Johnny's delight, Alan Deere suddenly appeared at Biggin Hill on 11 February. He had been taken off operations and, after a staff college course, sent to 13 Group Headquarters in Newcastle to fly a desk. Fortunately, the Senior Air Staff Officer there was his good friend Daddy Bouchier and (with Sailor's approval) he permitted Alan to spend a fortnight back in the front line. Johnny was happy to fly in his company again. One day, crossing the Channel east of Boulogne and circling behind Cap Gris Nez, 'we put up a couple of Huns just as if we were flushing partridge', but the New Zealanders were flying Spitfire Vbs and the Focke-Wulfs simply raced away from them.

Fortunately, the wing was being re-equipped at this time with the Spitfire IXb, a much-improved model which would give its pilots a better chance of competing on even terms with the Luftwaffe's best fighters. According to Alan, the IXb was markedly superior to the Fw 190 below 27,000 feet. Unlike the IXa, with which all other Spitfire IX squadrons in 11 Group were equipped, the IXb's supercharger came in at a lower altitude and the aircraft attained its best performance at 21,000 feet: at that height, it was about 50 kph faster than the Fw 190, better in the climb and much more manoeuvrable. 'As an all-round fighter,' Deere wrote, 'the Spitfire IXb was supreme, and undoubtedly the best mark of Spitfire produced, despite later and more powerful versions.' On 15 February, flying its new aircraft, the wing escorted twenty Liberator bombers to Dunkirk. German reaction, in the air and on the ground, was fierce: two Liberators were lost and eight damaged, but ten Focke-Wulfs were claimed as destroyed and Johnny clearly recalls the widespread exultation — and relief — among pilots and ground crews when they realised that the Spitfire IXb really was as good as rumour claimed it to be.

Dickie Milne, shot down and captured on 14 March, was replaced as Wing Commander Flying by Alan Deere, who had only just returned, most reluctantly, to his desk in Newcastle. During his long spell out of operations, Alan had thought deeply about wing tactics and was now able, with the support of Sailor Malan — whom he considered the best fighter tactician and leader produced by the Royal Air Force in the Second World War — to put his thoughts into practice.

Alan wanted squadron sections and squadrons within the wing to be independent yet inter-dependent. He would control the overall formation only insofar as routes and timings were concerned: 'the squadron and section leaders being free to act on their own initiative to engage enemy aircraft on sighting, first warning me that they intend to break formation.' He was keen to get away from 'mass-controlled attack and to rely on mutual support between the squadrons and sections within the wing as the tactical basis of a more flexible and profitable form of attack.' He introduced the finger four formation instead of the line-astern formation, much stricter R/T discipline and, above all, 'I stressed my belief that no matter what type of escort we undertook the wing must not be tied to the bomber speeds. Naturally, on close escort duties it was important to be always in sight of the bombers but the accepted tactic of flying alongside them was outmoded; it gave the bomber pilots some measure of comfort, but no protection.' Johnny was relieved to see the last of line astern formations. 'The new doctrine,' he recalled, 'was that a section of four aircraft should fly nearly line abreast in two pairs, though at slightly different altitudes to cover each other's blind spots, and stick together, both for attack or defence. If one pair found itself alone, it would be well advised to find some friends or go home, but if one partner in a pair lost his mate, he *must* clear off home as fast as he could go, because a single fighter — British or German — was a dead duck still flying.'

Although poor weather in March and April often prevented raids across the Channel, Alan welcomed the chance to introduce his new tactics and practise them intensively before the return of good fighting weather in the summer. Under Alan Deere, thought Johnny, 'junior pilots at last had a decent chance of living long enough to become useful' and he himself soon became more than that. During April, Jack Charles became Commanding Officer of 611 Squadron and Johnny a flight commander, in charge of B Flight. Charles was a Canadian and Johnny remembered him as a 'rather fearsome fellow, very aggressive, with exceptional eyesight'. 'Both had been appointed on my recommendation', wrote Deere, 'and both were to prove invaluable as supporting leaders in the months ahead.' At about this time, Johnny was described by one senior officer as, 'A reliable leader and skilful pilot who was as keen a fighter as he was modest in his claims.'

This recognition was gratifying, but he was acutely aware that he had not yet achieved a single confirmed victory in aerial combat. His eyesight, he knew, was very good. However, he remembered reading about an old chap in New Zealand whose sight gradually weakened until the day came when he could no longer read even newspaper headlines. He would sit on his front verandah, staring for hours at the clouds rolling overhead and willing himself to see their movements. After a couple of months, he could read small print without spectacles. Whatever the truth of this story, it inspired Johnny to believe that with regular exercise he could so strengthen his eye muscles that he would be able to spot aircraft at a greater distance and (just as important) for a longer period. He was too self-conscious to discuss this belief with anyone and so, whenever he was off operations in daytime, he would quietly slip away alone from Biggin Hill in his Spitfire and watch aircraft circling, taking off and landing. He would fly until he lost sight of them, note his position, then turn back until he could see them again. To his surprise, he soon found that he could see more aircraft from much further away and for a longer time.

For relaxation, he often went to Oxted to see his friend John Ferguson and drink at the Hoskins Arms there: 'Oxted became more of a home to me than a place to visit,' Johnny wrote. London was no longer the attraction it had been in 1942, largely because of the Americans. Likeable enough individually, there were so many of them that they swamped all desirable haunts — and so well paid that they could buy everything in sight, not that there was much on offer in 1943.

Moreover, Johnny was unimpressed by the wildly extravagant victory claims made by the gunners of American bombers. On 5 April, for example, having helped to escort a raid on Antwerp, he commented in his log book: 'Yanks claim seventy enemy fighters. Liars.' René Mouchotte, commander of 341 (Alsace) Squadron (which replaced 340 Squadron at Biggin Hill in March) shared his opinion. The Flying Fortresses, René wrote, 'always return with impressive figures of Boche shot down, which make us say ironically that in reality it is the Americans who are protecting us. It is not unusual for them to declare a figure of fifty to sixty Fw 190s shot down while we fighters have only seen a dozen and shot down one or two. Our orders are not to go too close for they often fire on us: one more victim to record.' According to a detailed history of the U.S. Eighth Air Force, claims were, on average, 'six or seven times greater than the true destroyed figure'. Nevertheless, Johnny's figure of seventy refers to *two* days' claims, not one: forty-seven on 4 April and twenty-three next day.

Apart from Oxted, Johnny went for relaxation to Farnborough[1], a beautiful village not far from Biggin Hill. His friend Colloredo Mansfeld (the senior flight commander in 611 Squadron) was an Austrian who fled to the United States in the early thirties, married a Canadian, returned to England to fight the Nazis and now rented a magnificent house in Farnborough. Collie was a wealthy man: 'in fact, he gave me a little motor car, an MG. I wish to goodness I had it now!' recalls Johnny sadly. Farnborough was quite unspoiled and he had many a pleasant meal there. The food, of course, was plain and there was little of it, but the service was superb: 'a real breath of peacetime.' He was introduced to snuff

1. Farnborough in Kent, not to be confused with Farnborough in Hampshire, which housed the Royal Aircraft Establishment. Ed.

and, as in Oxted, got to know many of the local people. A country-man himself, brought up in a small, quiet community where there was always time for an unhurried chat, he found rural England very much to his taste, especially in contrast to the hectic pace of his working day. Rural England occasionally reminded him too sharply of home, when parcels and letters arrived from his family and friends; especially parcels and letters from Natalie Grover. His fits of depression, of longing for a life and love that could not be in the foreseeable future, were intense but brief. He had little time, fortunately, to brood and he was, in any case, gifted with a robust temperament and resolved to enjoy each day to the full because it might well be the last. But looking back on those days, he says: 'I wish now that I had written more regularly to my sweetheart.'

He, Alan and Sailor used to hunt for partridge and pheasant on the eastern side of Biggin Hill. Johnnie Johnson, now com-manding a wing at Kenley, was almost as famous a shot as he was a fighter pilot, and managed to join one of these expeditions. His forceful, cheerful personality brightened some dull days, either in the field or whenever he came over to Biggin Hill for lunch. Game birds were none too common, but three or four determined hunters usually managed to bring down half a dozen birds be-tween them. When it came to eating the catch, however, Sailor preferred birds to hang, according to the customs of England, for longer than either of the New Zealanders thought wise and there were some vigorous debates on this point, all serving both to cement their good fellowship and take their minds off more serious matters.

Ken Branson, an Australian pilot in 611 Squadron, remembers Johnny as tense and edgy on the ground, refusing to stand down from any operation unless directly ordered to by his commanding officer. In the air, he was an aggressive leader, always looking for trouble. On fine, quiet days he would ring Group Headquarters and volunteer to carry out a weather reconnaissance over Le Havre. 'Come on, Aussie,' he would say, 'let's see if anyone's offering.' While Ken nervously scanned the sky, 'Johnny would do a few towering loops or rolls off the top a couple of miles off shore. He was confident that if anyone came up, we would clobber them with our height advantage or if there were too many of them we could easily dive to the north and home. I didn't always share his confidence though I had a lot of faith in his abilities and experience.' According to Ken, Johnny had a reputation for losing his wingman (his No. 2), but Johnny rejects this criticism firmly. 'It was my job to lead,' he says, 'and the wingman's to follow. He was there to watch my back, not me to watch his; that way, none of us would ever have shot a German down. We'd have been so busy looking at each other that the bloody Huns would have bagged us both.'

On 17 April Johnny had one of his busiest fighting days. In the morning, 611 Squadron was scrambled to 30,000 feet over Dungeness and then sent to sweep over Saint-Omer, diverting German attention from a bombing raid elsewhere. 'Intercepted by forty Huns,' he recorded later in his log book, 'and a terrific dogfight took place off Dunkirk. No loss to us.' That afternoon, after a hasty lunch, he was flying again. Alan Deere, having learned that a famous Luftwaffe commander (Walter Oesau) had recently moved to Tricqueville airfield, just south of the Seine Estuary, decided to welcome him with a surprise visit. He led the wing southward across the Channel from Dungeness at sea level until a point some fifteen kilometres off that estuary was reached. The Spitfires then climbed rapidly (to avoid coastal flak), crossed the coast east of Deauville, dived to tree-top height and raced towards Tricqueville. Fifteen kilometres short of the target, Mouchotte's squadron broke away eastward, climbing to 3,000 feet to guard against attack from another German airfield at Evreux while Deere and 611 Squadron were visiting Walter Oesau. He and his pilots fled just in time, leaving the British only an 'empty airfield and a miserable-looking hangar to fire at' before Mouchotte warned them that other enemies were on the way. 'The danger from collision,' thought Alan Deere of the next few minutes, 'was greater than from Hun bullets as Spitfires and Focke-Wulfs wove a chaotic pattern in the congested air space over the airfield.' The wing claimed two Fw 190s destroyed and two damaged in exchange for two Spitfires lost, both from the French squadron. 'Boy, that was some fight,' said Johnny to Alan afterwards. 'I'll bet the Hun ground crews at Tricqueville had a grandstand view. Pity we had to pull out, those Huns seemed keen.' Alan thought Johnny destroyed a German fighter, but he made no claim that day.

Though exhilarating, such missions were extremely dangerous and casualties mounted. All told, he flew thirty-three hours during April: a busy month, but May proved even busier. On the 3rd, he took part in a sweep over Boulogne intended to divert attention from a raid on an electrical power house at Amsterdam by eleven Ventura bombers of 487 (New Zealand) Squadron. Although he engaged several Fw 190s, hitting one certainly and probably two others, his pleasure in these efforts turned to dismay on learning that ten of the bombers had been shot down, among them that of Squadron Leader Leonard Trent, who would be awarded the Victoria Cross for bravely pressing home his attack.

Times were changing, Alan Deere reflected while en route to the target one day: 'eighty Fortresses as against the customary dozen or so 2 Group Bostons. This was the real thing; a punch that could be felt.' By May a dreadful routine was fully established: fighter sweeps, bomber escorts and diversion missions, all carried out in the teeth of fierce ground fire and unpredictable challenges from the Luftwaffe — one day, not a German fighter would be seen; next day, the sky would be full of them. 'Never have we flown so far with so little petrol,' wrote René Mouchotte, 'the prospect of prolonged aerial combat leaves us with the further prospect of a dip in the North Sea. . . How much water, water, there is to cross!'

Early in May, according to the newspapers, there was an air of suppressed excitement at Biggin Hill as the official victory tally of stations in that Sector (Hawkinge, West Malling, Gravesend, Lympne and Biggin Hill itself) neared the 1,000 mark. The first victory had been achieved three and a half years earlier, in November 1939. The BBC, represented by Gilbert Harding, arranged to make a sound recording; newspaper reporters were in constant attendance; and the Air Ministry's public relations staff were never off the telephone. Whoever brought down the thousandth enemy aircraft would win a sweepstake worth 300 pounds and the New Zealand press speculated patriotically on the prospects of Alan Deere or Johnny Checketts, the only New Zealand pilots then at Biggin Hill, collecting this fortune. As it happened, they both came tantalisingly close. On 15 May, when the score stood at 998, Deere rang Alan Mitchell (the New Zealand War Correspondent in London), inviting him to Biggin Hill because he felt certain that the target would be reached that day. He also invited Sailor Malan to fly.

Twelve Bostons were to bomb Caen airfield in the late afternoon and the Biggin Hill wing was to act as withdrawal cover. At 21,000 feet, the Spitfires swept in over Fécamp, swung round behind Le Havre, crossed the Seine Estuary and approached Caen from the east. On approaching the target area, Deere could just make out the retreating bombers and their close escorts. A little later, below and to port, he saw two Fw 190s climbing hard out of the haze. Since Jack Charles was leading the section (including Johnny) on that side, he ordered him to attack. Later, when they were all safely on the ground again, Charles described what happened next. 'I was just about to break away when you sang out,' he told Deere. 'It looked as if they were going down under the bombers with the idea of coming up and catching them from underneath. They were in line astern and I chased them. I don't think they saw me, they turned right into my sights. I could see bits of stuff flying off the first in all directions. . . Then the pilot baled out. I just flew straight on and got the other one. He didn't even turn. He blew clean up and went straight down.' Although Johnny had no opportunity to fire himself, he was perfectly placed to confirm Jack's account and did so enthusiastically.

Meanwhile, René Mouchotte had also been in action: 'a nice little job slid under my starboard wing,' he wrote. 'As I dived after my National Socialist, for I could see his black crosses shining now, I gave rapid orders over the radio so that my faithful troops would cover my attack. . . I got the nose gently into position and opened up. The great distance between us gave me little hope. But I was somewhat startled by what I saw: there was a violent explosion in the fuselage of the Focke-Wulf, followed by a huge flame. The plane rose in the air, then burst into bits, seeming to disintegrate in the air. The return to Biggin Hill,' he added, 'would have made all the gossiping *concierges* of Paris pale with envy. Never was the radio so loud with useless chatter.' Once on the ground, René gravely drew a diagram on the back of an envelope. 'I came in here,' he said, doodling with his pencil, 'he just went pouff.'

These three victories certainly brought up the magic figure, but their precise sequence could not be determined and it was therefore wisely decided to split the money and the honour be-tween Jack Charles and René Mouchotte. 'Thus it came about,' wrote Alan Deere, 'that the 1000th enemy aircraft destroyed by pilots operating from Biggin Hill was shared by a Canadian [who was born in England] and a Frenchman, while a South African station commander and a New Zealand wing leader looked on.'

Quite by chance, René Mouchotte had organised an enormous ball in the Hyde Park Hotel for that very night. The top brass in Fighter Command and many eminent Free French personalities, including General de Gaulle himself, were present. 'London no longer sees balls on such a scale and in such style,' recorded René proudly, but 'it was exactly what I needed to "launch" the "Alsace" Squadron [which he had formed in January] in London society.' A more than good time was had by all, but the wing was still airborne at 10.30 a.m. next morning. The official celebration of the great deed was an even grander ball at Grosvenor House, Park Lane, early in June. Over a thousand men and women attended, among them the heads of Fighter and Bomber Commands; three Royal Air Force bands provided music and the 'legendary Wind-mill Girls', as René described them, 'in on all the Biggin Hill par-ties (for some mysterious reason), gave one of their little numbers'. For once, in wartime Britain, the food and drink were of peacetime quality and quantity. 'Hundreds of ducks, chickens, lobsters, perfectly prepared,' recalled René, 'gorgeous side-dishes, beer, cocktails, champagne, all generously served.' Three large lobsters were specially dressed and labelled Hitler, Göring and Mussolini.

Vickers-Armstrongs, makers of the Spitfire, were said to have footed the bill — £2,500 — for what was, by general con-sent, the most splendid occasion of the war; an occasion doubly marked for Sailor Malan, whose wife gave birth to their second child only a few hours earlier. The highlight of the evening, as far as Alan Deere was concerned, was an unexpected gesture by a group of London taxi drivers who arrived en masse just before the ball officially ended, to offer their services free of charge to the pilots and their guests. A week later, Malan returned the com-pliment when he invited fifty cabbies to be guests at Biggin Hill. They arrived in a fleet of cabs, the leader carrying a grandfather clock strapped to the roof. 'This, together with a steering wheel suitably inscribed, the cabbies solemnly presented to the Mess as a memento of their visit, and both are proudly displayed in the Officers' Mess today.'

Colin Hodgkinson had joined 611 Squadron on 25 May, just four years after a mid-air collision which cost him both legs. He and Douglas Bader were the only two pilots to fly on operations in World War II after suffering such grievous injuries. During the past five months, Colin had served with three squadrons in Tangmere Sector before joining 'the first eleven', as he put it, at Biggin Hill. He flew in Johnny's flight and later described him as 'a genial, extroverted New Zealander who took the war in his stolid, canny stride. Kindly and efficient on the ground, he was a real "tradesman" on operations. It gave me great confidence to be under Checketts' wing, literally and figuratively.' For his part, Johnny remembered Colin as a very keen pilot, determined (like Bader) to show that he was at least as good as the next man, despite his handicap. Had he ever been obliged to bale out over the Channel, however, he would have found it very difficult to scramble into a dinghy. As it happened, Colin avoided that hazard, but his war ended in November when he made a forced landing in France and was captured. 'He liked a drink or two, did old Colin, and we had some jolly evenings together. I greatly admired the way he got about so well, in the air and on the ground. We soon learned to take no notice of his tin legs and that, I'm sure, is the way he wanted it.'

Johnny achieved his first confirmed victory in aerial combat on 30 May, having damaged at least four Fw 190s earlier that month. It was the squadron's hundredth victory of the war and earned him twenty pounds which went towards yet another celebration: life at Biggin Hill in 1943 was sadly short for all too many brave young men, but was lived to the full while it lasted. The wing had been ordered to cover Hawker Typhoon ground-attack aircraft bombing a power station at Caen. Two Fw 190s attacked Johnny and his No. 2, 'but we outclimbed them and they lost sight of us' as they manoeuvred to attack Blue 1 and 2, two Spitfires in another section. Johnny warned Blue 1 and then attacked the Fw 190 'from behind and below with a great overtaking speed. I opened fire from 200 metres. . . and saw heavy strikes on fuselage and wings. The enemy aircraft appeared to stop and shed cowlings and pieces and smoke in dense clouds. I broke upwards and saw him spin down smoking.' On the way home, he attacked another fighter head on over Fécamp; it fell away, apparently out of control, but with the Channel stretching ahead of him he was unable to follow it.

June brought him a substantive promotion to Flight Lieutenant and an honorary commission as a pilot in the Free French Air Force; it also brought long hours of daylight, numerous operations and two more confirmed victories. On the 21st he had a brief change from the routine of sweeps, scrambles and bomber escorts when he flew to Farnborough in Hampshire to take part in trials against a captured Fw 190. He was to escort the German fighter from there to Manston, Beachy Head, Tunbridge Wells and back to Farnborough, all at 25,000 feet: an altitude where the Spitfire IX usually had the advantage. The experiment both surprised and alarmed him. He took off after the Focke-Wulf and was supposed to catch up with it, but even flying beyond his maximum economical cruising speed was quite unable to do so. Worse still, when they landed, he learned that the pilot of the German fighter had not exceeded his maximum economical cruising speed. In future, he decided, he would fly his Spitfire much faster even on high level sweeps. He was allowed to fly the Focke-Wulf and found it a delightful aircraft. It had a wonderful rate of climb, it was very fast, its armament was formidable (four cannon and two heavy machine-guns, all beautifully-designed weapons, efficient and easy to service) and the gunsight seemed very effective. The Spitfire was hard to hold in a high speed dive whereas the Focke-Wulf was hard to pull out of a long, sustained dive: 'I've often wondered since how many German pilots killed themselves when going downhill very quickly.' Otherwise, he thought the two aircraft well matched except at high altitude, where both the Spitfire and the Messerschmitt 109 had a superior performance. However, Johnny found that in camera gun dogfights he easily overcame his Farnborough opponent in either the British or the German fighter not because he was a better *pilot* but because he was much more experienced in aerial combat. He drew what comfort he could from this discovery: the Spitfire IX and the Fw 190 were comparable aircraft and the difference between killing and being killed would lie in the hands of the men in the cockpits.

During his visit to Farnborough, Johnny met Wing Commander

Roland Winfield, a pilot-doctor greatly admired for his readiness to act as 'guinea pig' in many dangerous tests. One concerned the effects of catapulting Hurricanes from merchant ships. It had been supposed that pilots might not be able to stand the violent acceleration necessary to 'blast off' from the ship, but Roland himself volunteered to undertake trials which proved the technique reasonably safe. Another concerned the effects of lack of oxygen on aircrew at altitude: once again, he voluntarily risked his own life testing speculative theories. Sometimes Roland *chose* to fly on operations with bomber crews whose courage was in question. Johnny took to him at once, finding him modest and unassuming, like many brave men. They became friends and enjoyed a holiday together after the war in the South Island of New Zealand.

Meanwhile, Johnny returned to Biggin Hill and next day, 22 June, he took part in a most significant operation: the first American daylight raid on a target in the Ruhr. It cost the Americans heavy casualties — 169 airmen killed, wounded or captured; 16 Flying Fortresses destroyed and 75 damaged out of the 235 despatched — but from then on, the industrial heart of Germany was under constant attack by day and night. For this first raid, seven wings of Royal Air Force fighters covered the withdrawal, forming an umbrella over Sliedrecht in northern Holland, but the bombers had been heavily punished while outside Spitfire range by German fighters who pressed home their attacks fiercely. As the American bombers penetrated ever more deeply, the battle moved with them and the Royal Air Force wing leaders 'found themselves groping in the rear,' as Alan Deere recalled, 'unable to reach the main battle area', despite carrying an external fuel tank that could be jettisoned.

The summer was therefore spent mainly in escorting medium bombers — Mitchells, Venturas, Bostons and Marauders — attacking targets in France and the Low Countries. By no means as destructive as the Fortresses or Liberators, they nevertheless caused much more damage than the light bombers of 1941 and provoked sufficient reaction from German fighters to keep the Biggin Hill wing fully occupied. There were few days when Johnny was not involved, either protecting bombers or seeking out enemy fighters; and every day the flak grew more intense and accurate: 'it was often so good that I could see the red explosion flame and hear the shell explode, but to my surprise I was not seriously hit, nor could I later find more than a few holes and scratches.' He greatly admired the skill and resolution of bomber pilots, British and American, and never ceased to thank his lucky stars that he was not one of them: 'because although we always escorted them into their bombing area, we could then pull away and gain altitude to avoid the flak, whereas the poor old bombers had to carry straight on, right through it.' By the end of June, he had another thirty-seven hours in his log book, making a grand total of 196 for the first six months of 1943; rather more than one a day. In that time, he successfully completed exactly one hundred operations.

Johnny then learned, to his intense disappointment, that 611 Squadron was being taken out of the line and sent to Coltishall near Norwich in Norfolk for a rest. He hated the thought of leaving 'dear old Biggin Hill', to say nothing of his good friends, service and civilian, and the many pleasant places around Biggin Hill where he had learned to take all the rest and relaxation he needed from frontline action. But there was nothing for it, 'orders is orders', so he packed up and prepared to leave. He was, however, surprised to learn that 485 (New Zealand) Squadron would come from Tangmere to Biggin Hill to replace them — and also annoyed, because he believed that 611 Squadron was no more in need of a rest than the New Zealanders, who were already in the front line at Tangmere. To add insult to injury, they would swap their inferior Spitfire Vbs for 611's excellent Mark IXs. While he and his mates were standing about, waiting to leave and brooding upon injustice, Jack Charles (the squadron commander) came up and said: 'You're not coming with us, Checks old son; you're to stay here and take over this lot', meaning 485 Squadron. Johnny thought this joke in poor taste and said so, warmly. Charles, never a man to flinch from any challenge, replied sharply and within moments angry words were flying freely. Johnny stormed off to see Malan and Deere and learned that Charles was not joking. He was so upset at leaving 611 Squadron that it was some time before the good news sank in: he was to be promoted to Squadron Leader; he was to command New Zealand's own fighter squadron, the squadron in which he had begun his career as a humble Pilot Officer; best of all, he was to stay at Biggin Hill.

In Alan Deere's opinion, 'Johnny was a good pilot, no better, but he was an exceptional shot. . . Although he was older by far than the average fighter pilot, one never thought of him as a father figure. He was, if anything, boyish to a degree. I know when I first met him at Kenley in 1941, when I was a Squadron Leader and he a Pilot Officer of twenty-nine years to my twenty-four years, I looked upon him as a younger man — his outlook was refreshingly that way.' Nevertheless, his powers of command developed so quickly that Deere had no hesitation in promoting him over a number of his more senior contemporaries. 'There was at the time a lot of ill-feeling about the appointment,' he recalled, 'but I am pleased to say that after a few short months in command the pilots of 485 Squadron would have followed him anywhere. His success in the air was reflected in the squadron's better kill-rate which until he took command had been poor.'

That ill feeling was not shared (or even mentioned) by Doug Brown. 'We have got Johnny Checketts as C.O.,' he wrote on 12 July 1943, 'which in my opinion is a great thing, as he has got plenty of what it needs and will bring the squadron back to the Reg Grant standard.' As for its kill-rate, 485 Squadron (like all fighter squadrons) had long spells out of the firing line or in employment where opportunities for aerial combat were few. Even so, it claimed only six enemy aircraft destroyed during the fourteen months before Johnny took command. He would lead the squadron for not quite ten weeks (the shortest tenure of its nine wartime commanders) and yet, employing the sensible tactics he had been taught by Malan and Deere, 485 Squadron was credited in that time with the destruction of more enemy aircraft than any other unit in 11 Group: eighteen confirmed and three probables in exchange for the loss of only seven pilots — three of whom, including himself, would make their way back to England.

## CHAPTER SEVEN

# Commanding: 485 Squadron at Biggin Hill, July to September 1943

Marty Hume and Garry Barnett, Johnny's flight commanders, would support him loyally and ably in their different ways. Marty was 'a terrific chap', in Johnny's opinion: a real livewire, full of good humour and very well liked by everyone, pilots and ground crews. Garry, less outgoing than Marty, was an extremely good organiser and 'the steadiest fellow you could ever wish to serve with'. Both men would later become squadron commanders themselves. 'Old Checks had his faults,' recalled Marty in March 1985, 'as we all did, but the fellow was a genuine, and did not overclaim as so many did; but he had very little psychology and he trod on a lot of fellows' pet corns and got himself unpopular.'

There are, of course, times — especially on active military service — when pet corns must suffer and popularity, in itself, is not a prime requirement for a successful military commander. Nevertheless, one may doubt if Marty's opinion as to Johnny's unpopularity was widely shared. 'He was certainly not unpopular,' wrote Doug Brown in October 1985, 'but it would be an exceptional situation if he did not offend some pilots in his squadron, for it must be appreciated that there were many who, under the stresses suffered, became temperamental.' Leslie White thought Johnny world class as a fighter pilot, and greatly admired his courage and determination to get in close. 'He fought for the betterment of others without a thought about his own life.' In Ken Lee's opinion, the fact that he was older than most fighter pilots had something to do with his aggression. 'I always thought of him as impulsive and excitable both in the air and on the ground. Once having embarked on a course of action, he pursued it relentlessly. Perhaps partly because of this he was at times a difficult man to follow in the air and on occasions even experienced pilots were unable to stay with him.'

According to Laddie Lucas (an outstanding fighter pilot of World War II), if one were to ask a dozen senior officers which, of all the commands they had had in the service, was 'the most pleasing, the most satisfying, the most stimulating,' each would probably answer: 'Commanding a squadron in wartime.' The Wing Commander Flying could say how he wished the squadrons to fly in his wing, but could not meddle with their internal affairs. 'If he didn't like the way your squadron was performing, he had a remedy in his own hands — to have you posted.' Everyone in a fighter squadron, from the two flight commanders down to the most junior fitter or rigger or orderly room clerk, depended on the squadron leader both on the ground and in the air. A squadron, though large enough to make its weight felt in combat, was also small enough to enable its commander to know everyone in it. 'An able C.O. of a fighter squadron,' Laddie concluded, 'could make a mark with it and lift it well above the average in the sector, in the group, in the command, in a month; under a poor commander it would slip quickly down the league table. Either way, things happened very fast. That was the devil of it. The fact was that in wartime a fighter squadron was as good or as indifferent as its commanding officer.' Duncan Smith agreed: 'Command of an operational squadron,' he wrote, 'is the high point of an RAF career. Promotion may bring wider responsibilities, but never the same satisfaction.'

Johnny was told that his squadron would probably remain 'in the line' for no longer than three months before being rested, but these would be summer months and operations of one sort or another would therefore be flown on every possible day. Although this news pleased him, he was apprehensive about taking over his old squadron because it still contained several pilots who had been senior to him when he first joined it at Kenley in November 1941. Both Sailor Malan and Alan Deere bluntly told him to forget his apprehensions. They reckoned he was the best man available and it was their job — not his — to decide such matters. He was to stop wittering and get on with it. If he let them down, they swore never to go hunting or boozing with him again.

Faced with such dire threats, Johnny swore — privately — to do everything in his power to make his squadron the best at Biggin Hill, if not the best in Fighter Command. He began by standing it down for three days while the New Zealanders were trained in Biggin Hill tactics. 'We had finally seen the last of the weaving formation,' wrote Johnnie Houlton, 'and from now on flew in the "finger four" battle formation, which was simple and practical. In that same month (July 1943), Laddie Lucas, newly-appointed wing leader at Coltishall in Norfolk, was also getting rid of line astern flying. 'Operationally,' he wrote, 'nothing but line abreast would, in future be tolerated.' There can be no doubt that the line astern system cost Fighter Command many avoidable casualties. Why it was not abolished sooner, given the vehement objection to it among experienced combat pilots, is a question not as yet sufficiently investigated.

During July, the wing carried out many bomber escorts and on two or three occasions when Alan Deere was forced to turn back, Johnny had the exhilarating experience of leading the wing. When Alan went on leave later in the month, René Mouchotte of 341 Squadron acted as wing leader. As always, the presence of bombers, especially if they threatened airfields, provoked a fierce reaction from German fighters and Johnny was regularly involved in desperate dogfighting. At about 8.45 a.m. on 14 July, while leading his squadron as cover for 140 Fortresses attacking Le Bourget airfield, Paris, he spotted a solitary Fw 190 far below flying towards Le Havre. Suspecting a trap, he checked the sky carefully, saw nothing to alarm him and led a section of four Spitfires to the attack. He got close enough to see his enemy's yellow nose and tail (contrasting sharply with grey-green camouflage on wings and fuselage) before the pilot realised his danger and dived away at high speed. Johnny fired a long burst from about 400 metres, seeing several brilliant flashes on the yellow tail. By then, however, he had dropped 12,000 feet in only a few seconds and blacked out momentarily as he pulled out of his dive; when he recovered, the German had gone.

On the following afternoon, leading the squadron home over the Forêt de Crécy at 20,000 feet, he saw five Fw 190s about 5,000 feet below flying south, straight and level, in the direction of Fécamp. They spotted the Spitfires at the same moment and turned north towards Cap Gris Nez. Johnny ordered his section and one other (eight fighters in all) to attack, covered from above by the third section. No sooner had the attack begun than a pack of at least fifteen Focke-Wulfs jumped the New Zealanders and Johnny realised that he had been neatly ambushed. Keeping his voice calm and flat, he called down his own covering section and asked the Frenchmen of 341 Squadron (whom he knew to be nearby) for help. In no time at all, there were aircraft everywhere, twisting and turning and firing. He managed to close to within 100 metres of one German fighter, firing hard, and saw strikes on the port wing close to the fuselage; suddenly, it rolled over and went straight down with flames streaming from its belly, crashing on the beach just north of the Somme Estuary. He knew that he was now too low for safety — one always lost precious height in combat — and so he ordered the New Zealanders to climb. His own wingman, Flight Sergeant Terry Kearins, failed to climb hard enough and his engine was hit. Johnny saw it streaming glycol and urged Terry to bale out, but it was too late: a Focke-Wulf sent him down in flames just east of the forest. (Terry, in fact, *did* get out, unseen by Johnny, and the two would meet again, a few weeks later, in France.) Meanwhile, the pilot of Johnny's victim had taken to his parachute and was being guarded during his descent by another Focke-Wulf. Johnny tried to get at this aircraft, but was forced away and decided to call it a day; he gathered his squadron and turned for home without further loss or injury.

Major Jim Haun and Captain J. R. (Pappy) Walker were two American pilots serving with a Tactical Reconnaissance squadron in the United States Army Air Force who were farmed out, as Jim puts it, to a Royal Air Force fighter squadron to gain combat experience. They joined 485 Squadron in July. Pappy Walker, unfortunately, was killed on the 14th, but Jim Haun survived. 'We were woefully unprepared for combat,' Jim recalls, but Johnny decided to employ Jim as his own wingman. 'I explained that I had no experience in aerial gunnery. Johnny said: "No problem. Just shove your gun barrels up his arse and pull the trigger." This sounded reasonable to me, but I discovered that you had to *see* them before you could perform that trick . . . Johnny had eyes like a hawk. He must have had 20/20 vision. He could spot them at great distances in the dark sky at altitude. I never could.'

An excellent pilot, Jim flew with Johnny as his wingman when René Mouchotte led the wing to Tricqueville in the late afternoon of 27 July, escorting eighteen Marauder bombers. Johnny, leading his squadron, noticed fourteen Fw 190s following him at the same level. Doug Brown, in a letter home, described what happened next: 'Johnny called out to us "throttle back and let them catch up" which we did, and when they were nearly in range, we opened up and climbed like blazes leaving poor old Jerry nicely below. Then the fun started.' With Jim Haun guarding his rear, Johnny dived below an enemy fighter and came up behind it at close range. Taking his time, he aimed carefully. Pieces flew off the cowling and black smoke billowed out of the engine; the fighter rolled slowly over and another careful burst sent it diving down in flames, as Jim would later confirm.

In the ensuing mêlée, however, Johnny became isolated and therefore climbed as hard as he could to 30,000 feet. Over the French coast, he spotted two Fw 190s about 5,000 feet below him and promptly attacked; when he was already committed, he realised that there were in fact *three* enemy aircraft and that he might not live long to regret his rashness. He fired at one, seeing strikes on the port wing; the second took evasive action and he destroyed the third: 'When I last saw him,' Johnny later reported, 'he was going down steeply with flames streaming from the fuselage and cockpit.' It was a brilliant action, part of an excellent day for the Biggin Hill wing: in all, nine Fw 190s were claimed as destroyed for no British losses. Next day, several congratulatory signals were received: one from the Prime Minister, one from Sir Trafford Leigh-Mallory (head of Fighter Command), another from Hugh Saunders (head of 11 Group) and, not least, one from the women who worked in the Operations Room at Fighter Command Headquarters.

On the morning of 28 July, Johnny landed at Coltishall after escorting a dozen Bostons to Amsterdam. He felt so tired that he could hardly climb out of the cockpit. The flak had been heavy and accurate throughout the mission, causing him to throw his Spitfire all over the sky, and he had had a hard fight with a well-flown Me 109; some of his shots must have struck home, because he saw smoke trailing from it as his opponent dived away. Tired or not, he knew that he had to fly twice more that day, covering the withdrawal of Flying Fortresses from a raid on Germany, and escorting eighteen Marauders to Tricqueville. He toyed with an unappetising lunch and then tried to relax, sitting in the sun outside the mess. No-one had anything to say, but no-one could rest properly either. Their ears were still filled with the morning's uproar and their brains were reminding them of their secret terrors, now that they had nothing to do. When take-off time came, Johnny learned that his aircraft had not been re-armed. This obviously vital job normally took about ten minutes, but the armourers had not got around to it in two hours. He was furious. Worse still, he allowed his fury to get the better of his commonsense and took off with an unarmed Spitfire. This was undoubtedly the single most stupid act of his entire career and recognition of his stupidity, which came to him within minutes of taking off, did nothing to improve his temper. Nevertheless, he drew a lesson from it, as he tried to do from all his experiences. Many pilots, he thought, both British and German, got themselves killed not because they came up against a better man but because tiredness made them careless or silly. He knew he was tired and must therefore make a conscious effort to stay calm and concentrate all the time; he could do nothing about meeting a better man, but he could avoid killing himself.

On 31 July, with these thoughts still fresh in mind, Johnny led his squadron yet again to Tricqueville, escorting a formation of Marauder bombers. Observing fourteen enemy fighters manoeuvring to attack the bombers, he ordered two of his sections to attack while he covered them with the third section. After a few minutes, he noticed two Me 109s orbiting away from the battle area, presumably waiting to pick off damaged stragglers. They did not realise that they were themselves vulnerable stragglers until Johnny and his three companions fell on them. One promptly fled, but

Johnny trapped the other. Guarded by his wingman (Peter Gaskin) he fastened on to its tail, forcing it down to ground level, skilfully following its every twist and turn until he managed to land a stream of cannon shells full in the cockpit. The Messerschmitt struck the top branches of some apple trees, fell into the orchard and skidded into a barn, moving it at least seventy-five metres before it collapsed around the fighter, 'the whole lot blazing furiously'. Having checked that the sky was now clear and that Peter Gaskin was still on guard, he took a leisurely cine film of the blaze.

That evening, on returning tired but happy to Biggin Hill, Johnny learned that he had been awarded the Distinguished Flying Cross. The citation reads: 'This officer has led the squadron and, on occasions the wing, with great skill. He has invariably displayed great keenness to engage the enemy and has destroyed two enemy aircraft and damaged several more. In addition, he has destroyed two E-boats and successfully attacked military installations.' These words naturally delighted him and so, too, did a public tribute from Alan Deere: 'Squadron Leader Checketts,' he said, 'is among the best commanding officers who have led the new Zealand Spitfire Squadron.' He also received a telegram offering 'heartiest congratulations on your gong and very best wishes from all in 611.' 'Johnny Checketts got his DFC yesterday,' wrote Doug Brown in a letter to his family in New Zealand, 'which he more than deserves as he has now seven destroyed. Jolly good fighter pilot.' His victory on the 31st was indeed his seventh confirmed in addition to one probable and at least eight damaged. As for the E-boats, however, he made no personal claim: he was but one of four pilots attacking them and did not even see them sink.

August was a desperately busy month, as Alan Deere recalled it. 'Dawn found us over France as high cover to Marauders; late morning, in the Caen area covering our own 2 Group bombers; early afternoon, over Holland as withdrawal cover to Fortresses returning from Germany; and late evening, on a fighter sweep in the Pas de Calais area. In many ways the tempo of operations compared with that of August 1940, although the absence of those nerve-destroying hours on readiness made the task seem less arduous.'

Then, on 9 August, came one of the greatest days in Johnny's career. Late that afternoon, the Biggin Hill wing (led by Alan

Deere) escorted forty-eight Marauders bound for Saint-Omer. Something went amiss with the bombers' navigation and the formation split up, one group flying away from the target area towards Douai. Alan stayed with those still heading for Saint-Omer and ordered Johnny to cover the rest. These eventually dropped their bombs nowhere near the target, watched by 485 Squadron from high above. As the bombers turned for home, Johnny called Alan, using their code names: 'Brutus from Jubilee Leader. Huns climbing from below, about four I think. I don't think they've seen us. Can I attack?' 'What's your position, Jubilee Leader?' replied Alan. 'Between Saint-Omer and the coast, coming out.' 'OK, Johnny, attack with one section [four fighters]. I'm returning at full speed to assist.' Johnny took his section down and silence followed until Alan heard him say: 'Come on, Gibby, have a go. You, too, numbers 3 and 4.'

A few minutes later, he saw the section approaching him in perfect formation. 'How did you get on, Johnny?' he called and received a staggering reply. Johnny and his three companions had found not four but eight Me 109s. They were not stalking the bombers: instead, they were cruising along, line abreast, as if practising for a peacetime air display, with nothing worse to trouble them than a ragged formation or a bumpy landing. It was a perfect example of his own recent thought about carelessness killing more pilots than superior opponents. He remembered also the corollary — stay calm, concentrate — and quickly shot down three of the Messerschmitts; a fourth was probably destroyed, but he did not see it explode or crash. The three pilots who accompanied him (Jack Rae, Hugh Tucker and Bruce Gibbs) also claimed one each. Only one of the eight German pilots escaped unscathed in an action that lasted scarcely a minute and none of them even opened fire.

This truly unique feat, as Alan Deere described it, was made the subject of a BBC radio broadcast by Johnny (supported by Bruce Gibbs), re-broadcast in New Zealand and widely publicised in the press as the biggest single success in the squadron's history. Johnny's own contribution was 'believed to be a record for Fighter Command during an offensive sweep. Other pilots, of course, have shot down three or more in one flight, but in different types of action.' His official 'bag' was now ten, all obtained since 30 May. The Christchurch *Press* reported: 'This latest action of the New Zealanders is modern aerial warfare at its grimmest. It was fought at over four hundred miles an hour. The cannons were fired for a little over ten seconds while the actual fighting lasted for about a minute. It is true that the Germans were surprised, but then they paid the penalty for not keeping a strict lookout.'

Surviving German records confirm six of these seven claims: four fighters were totally destroyed and two force landed with thirty and ten percent damage respectively. All six went down in the Lille-St. Pol area. Johnny received telegrams from Sir Archibald Sinclair (Secretary of State for Air) congratulating him on his 'outstanding exploit' and from Hugh Saunders on his 'magnificent personal achievement and grand show put up by 485 today'. Group Captain A. J. M. Manson, Deputy AOC at Royal New Zealand Air Force Headquarters in London, wrote 'to offer the congratulations of the RNZAF. . . on the great effort of 485 Squadron over the last few weeks. New Zealand ought to be justifiably proud of the squadron as a whole, and I will be pleased if you will convey these sentiments to the personnel.' In Jim Haun's opinion, 'Johnny was very aggressive, but never reckless. The squadron pilots knew that he had exceptional eyesight that enabled him to manoeuvre the squadron into a favourable position to attack. He would then strike fast and hard.'

Less than two weeks later, however, the squadron suffered a blow almost as shattering as that which it had inflicted. On 22 August, while covering an attack by Marauder bombers on an airfield at Beaumont-le-Roger (south-west of Rouen) Johnny spotted a large force of enemy fighters approaching at the same altitude. Correctly anticipating a head-on attack, he ordered his pilots to hold formation, fly straight ahead and *meet* the attack head-on. A fighter presented a very small target seen from in front and closing speeds were so great that accurate shooting was extremely difficult. The head-on attack was, in fact, primarily intended to break up a formation. If the attacked fighters dived away, they were left vulnerable to a second — and more measured — attack from enemies holding a precious altitude advantage that could readily be converted into speed.

Tragically, Johnny's order was not obeyed. His pilots scattered in all directions and he found himself alone: safe, for the moment, but with the scene of action far behind him. Jack Rae, Mac Sutherland, Leslie White and Fraser Clark were all shot down, though only Clark was killed. Jack Rae, recommended by Johnny for a Bar to his DFC and due to be promoted and made a flight commander in another squadron next day, would spend the rest of the war as a prisoner. Mac Sutherland was also captured, badly wounded, and though he later escaped was re-captured and eventually repatriated. As for Leslie White (whom Johnny had recommended for a commission, gazetted on the very day he went missing), he got clean away and after many adventures returned to England. But all four had been experienced pilots and no squadron could long endure such losses. As for Johnny himself, he engaged an Me 109 and hit it several times, even though one of his cannons jammed. He got so close that oil from the German fighter spewed over his windscreen, obliging him to break away. Consequently, he did not see what became of it and could only claim it 'damaged' although privately he had little doubt that his opponent would not have got home. Next day, he destroyed an Fw 190 near Amiens and on the 24th acted as wing leader, escorting 86 Fortresses to Villacoublay airfield, near Paris.

René Mouchotte was killed on 27 August 1943: 'A man of great personality, respected by everyone,' wrote Johnny. 'He was sadly missed and we were all desolate at losing such a good chap.' More than three years earlier, after the fall of France and before he had even flown a British fighter, René had written: 'In spite of those who seek to stop me fighting for my country, in spite of my country herself, I am now committed to the crusade until victory or death. I regret nothing and I shall fight convinced of the greatness of the end I seek.' A tall man, slim and elegantly dressed, rarely seen without a long cigarette holder, his courteous though reserved manner was not at all typical of fighter pilots. He was, nevertheless, a strong commander and a most dangerous opponent. But by this time he was almost exhausted, as the last words of his diary reveal: 'The sweeps go on, at a terrible pace. . . I feel a pitiless weariness from them. . . The smallest effort gets me out of breath; I have a crying need of rest, were it even for forty-eight hours. I have not taken a week's leave for two years. Always at readiness to fly or stuck in the office on administrative work! Anyway, where can I go?. . . Tomorrow morning I am flying again.'

Rene's death, on his 408th offensive mission, harshly illustrated the truth of Johnny's belief that a single fighter could not long survive. His No. 2 (the pilot specially charged to protect his rear) on his last mission had been Pierre Clostermann, who lost contact with him and went after an Fw 190. Although Clostermann would later become a famous combat pilot, his flight commander had already had occasion to rebuke him sharply for losing his No. 1. As Alan Deere wrote, Clostermann 'should have been aware of the golden rule in the wing: a No. 2 must never lose his leader, the only exceptions being if he himself was shot down or had to pull out because of engine failure. This may sound a harsh rule, but it paid dividends.' Clostermann, having despatched his Fw 190, heard Mouchotte call 'I am alone', but no-one saw him alive again.

## CHAPTER EIGHT

# An Absorbing Manhunt (1): September, 1943

... the English amuse themselves by encumbering us with a quantity of small objects of undeniable usefulness 'if' fate should make us the quarry in some absorbing manhunt. More than once, I admit, I have thought about this kind of sport. It must be extraordinarily exciting ...

The Mouchotte Diaries, p. 188

Airmen whose duties took them across the Channel were regularly lectured by representatives of MI 9, the War Office branch concerned with Allied Prisoners of War, about what to do — and not do — should they find themselves crash landing or descending by parachute into Occupied Europe. We fly, wrote René Mouchotte, 'with our pockets stuffed with odd paraphernalia: compasses hidden almost everywhere in the form of trouser buttons, propelling pencils and collar studs; miniature hack-saw sewn into the belt; maps, on silk, of Holland, Belgium and France hidden in shoulder pads. We carry nutritive chocolate, pills to stop us going to sleep, an ampoule of morphine with a needle to inject it, tablets to purify water and a great deal of French and Belgian money. With all that, we are ready to face the terrors of a grand pursuit. . . .' Only ten days after René was killed, came Johnny's last operation from his beloved Biggin Hill. Luckier than René, he would experience the excitement — and misery — of an 'absorbing manhunt' without the opportunity to test the usefulness of this 'odd paraphernalia'. The selfless assistance of many perfect strangers proved of far more use to him.

Having already flown twice on 6 September, and with evening coming on, Johnny supposed the day's work over. He therefore arranged to go out to dinner and had changed into his best uniform when word unexpectedly came through that a high cover escort for Marauders attacking ammunition dumps in the marshalling yards at Serqueux was required. The Spitfires were just swinging away from the target when twenty Fw 190s dived on them out of the sun. The squadron broke up and dogfighting began. Johnny sent one of the Germans down in flames and pursued a second down to ground level, without managing to finish it off. He had used nearly all his ammunition and was making his way home with his No. 2 (Johnnie Houlton) when they were set upon by several enemy fighters. Houlton's call for help was heard by Alan Deere, who promptly turned back from the coast with his No. 2. They were unable to locate the scene of the fight, but Houlton later told them that Johnny had baled out.

'At the time,' wrote Alan Deere, 'it was to me a great personal loss; to the Biggin Wing a tragedy for Checketts was a real "ace" and a great inspiration to the younger pilots.' Now tired and ill, Alan was admitted to hospital nine days later and never flew on operations again. In four years of war, he had nearly 700 hours of operational flying to his credit and claimed twenty-two enemy aircraft destroyed, ten probably destroyed and eighteen damaged. Johnny, for his part, had flown about 450 operational hours by then and claimed thirteen destroyed, three probables and nine damaged, all while flying from Biggin Hill in 1943. Twenty-four of these successful combats came in the last eighteen weeks and all thirteen of his confirmed victories were achieved in the last hundred days.

On 6 September, however, Johnny was fighting for his own life. Bursts of flak had suddenly appeared around him and he weaved and twisted to avoid them. Then he saw five Fw 190s above him at three o'clock coming down to attack and warned Houlton. 'We fought for altitude and finally got it,' he later recalled, 'when, to my surprise, I saw two more Fw 190s above me. One of them came for me in a port turn, the same as mine, and the other took the other turn and attacked head on. The first enemy aircraft could not get me and I thought the other one could not either. His first attack was miles out and I thought I would get a shot at him next time round, but we both missed. His third attack was terrific and I saw all his cannon firing, also his spinner and engine cowlings. There was a terrific explosion at my feet and my cockpit filled with flames.'

Covered in blazing petrol, Johnny struggled to open the hood and bale out, but it refused to open. His oxygen mask and helmet were on fire and he forced himself to keep his eyes closed. He could feel pieces of rubber smouldering on his face and the smell of rubber, cloth and flesh burning was intolerable. Somehow, he got the hood open and struggled out of the cockpit as the Spitfire plunged into its last dive. The toe of his right boot caught on the hood catch inside the front windscreen and he was flung on to his back, lying for a moment along the fuselage. His eyes were still tightly shut because he could feel the heat of flames licking round his face and body. He was terrified of hitting the tail plane as he kicked himself clear of the cockpit and even more terrified that his parachute might have been burned. He opened his eyes, but at first could only see a white haze. Then he found that he could see his clothes, still smouldering, and the ground far below, but nothing to the side or above. He pulled the ripcord and to his great joy a canopy suddenly bloomed above him and checked his fall. He beat out the flames around his legs and arms, cursing that his best uniform was now ruined. Only then did he remember the war. 'The Fw 190 flew close to me and I was terribly afraid — would he shoot me? No. I saw my No. 2 fly away home to dinner as I drifted slowly down with my white canopy billowing above me and my friend the enemy watching me.'

As he slowly descended, he realised that the skin of his forehead had come away from the flesh and was hanging over his eyes. He pulled it away and found to his relief that he could see as well as ever. Now, for the first time, he began to feel pain. But he looked across the Channel to England — and Biggin Hill — and immediately resolved to avoid capture and get back there if he could, even though he did not yet know how badly injured he was. He was about ten kilometres west of Abbeville on the Somme and no more than twenty kilometres from the coast. The Sussex coast lay only a further eighty kilometres away; surely he could manage such a little journey? Fortunately, it did not occur to him at the time that Hitler had been failing to solve the same problem for the past three years.

For the time being, however, there was the more immediate problem of a field rushing swiftly towards him, full of peasants. He landed awkwardly, hurting his back, but scrambled quickly to his feet and gathered up his parachute. He tried to stuff it into a wheat-stook, watched by an elderly woman; the rest of the peasants simply got on with their work. It would not all go in, but he had neither the time nor the strength to make a proper job of hiding it. His Mae West was less trouble; it slid easily into another stook. No soldiers had yet appeared, although he had seen some clearly during his descent, and the peasants were neither helping nor hindering him. He looked around desperately for somewhere to hide, to bathe and bind up his wounds and find some different clothes: he could throw away his tattered uniform jacket, but his trousers were burnt away almost to the crotch and he would need something other than scorched flying boots on his feet.

As he stumbled towards a rough track leading away from the field, the elderly woman ran over to him, grabbed his arm and asked him (in French) if he was German. When she saw his Royal Air Force wings and realised he was English, she put her fingers in her mouth and gave a shrill whistle. A boy rode up on a bicycle and together they seated him on the back carrier. Although she spoke no English and Johnny knew no French, he soon understood that the boy was to take him to a small wood which he could now see about half à kilometre away. It was an agonising journey, perched precariously on the back of a bicycle with almost flat tyres, wobbling slowly along a rough track. All his burns and bruises were crying aloud for attention, but at least no bones seemed to be broken. The boy dropped him at the edge of the wood and rode off without a backward glance.

Almost at once Johnny heard the roar of a motorbike and scrambled hastily behind a small bush just as the bike came into sight, ridden by a German soldier. Even at that crisis in his affairs, he could not resist peeping out to see what make it was and finding, to his surprise, that it was a mere two-stroke. He had imagined that the Germans all rode those beautiful BMW four-stroke machines. It returned a few minutes later, the rider now balancing Johnny's parachute on his petrol tank. Sitting there, gasping with pain and beginning to suffer the shock of his narrow

Top: Ernest Checketts (left) with his family early in 1941: Johnny (right), Peggy and Alan.

Bottom left: Pilot Officer Checketts, commissioned at Wigram on 14 June 1941. He was officially considered 'A good average pilot who handles his aeroplane smoothly. He has dash but must guard against becoming over confident.'

Bottom right: Johnny with Al Deere's much-loved scots terrier Stevie (named for a friend killed during the Battle of Britain) at Kenley in east Surrey early in 1942. Deere was sent to the US at the end of January and Johnny cared for Stevie until Deere returned to England in May 1942. (RNZAF Research Collection, Wigram: MUS 000242)

*Top left:* Johnny playing with Stevie. Deere took command of 403 (Canadian) Squadron at Southend, Essex in May, so Johnny hopped into a Spitfire, set Stevie on his knee, and flew him down to Southend.

*Top right:* Johnny in front of his Spitfire at Biggin Hill in 1943. 'Poor old girl', he told me, 'she looks more battered than me.' This is the photograph he would sign and send to autograph-hunters.

*Bottom:* Painting by John Chrisp of Johnny in action on 9 August 1943. Leading a section of four Spitfires, he attacked eight Me 109s, shooting down three and perhaps a fourth; his three fellow-pilots claimed one each. The action lasted scarcely a minute and not one of the Germans even opened fire.

*Top:* Bill Jordan (left) New Zealand's High Commissioner in London, with Johnny, Bruce Gibbs, Jack Rae and Hugh Tucker at Biggin Hill, shortly after their astonishing feat on 9 August 1943: between them they destroyed four Me 109s and damaged at least two others out of a formation of eight over Lille-St. Pol. *(IWM 28177)*

*Left:* Agnès de Nanteuil of Vannes in Brittany, who helped Johnny and Terry Kearins to evade the Germans in October 1943. Arrested by the Gestapo in March 1944, shot while attempting to escape in August, she died in a cattle truck a week later, aged twenty-one.

*Right*: Terry Kearins (left), Johnny and Libby at the Levanant farm, near Vannes, in October 1943.

*Below:* Johnny and Al Deere, one of the RAF's most famous fighter pilots (who was also a South Islander, born in Westport) at the Central Gunnery School, Sutton Bridge, Lincolnshire, in December 1943. 'Any success I had either in combat or leading,' said Johnny, 'I owe to my good friend Al, who taught me all I know.' *(RNZAF, Wigram, MUS 03047)*

*Top:* Johnny as Wing Leader (commanding three squadrons of Spitfires, one British, one Polish and one Canadian) at Horne, Kent, on or about D-Day, 6 June 1944. *(RNZAF, Wigram, MUS 031197)*

*Bottom left:* Natalie Grover, later Johnny's wife, in June 1944.

*Bottom right:* Portrait of Johnny as he looked in 1945 on his return to New Zealand, made by Maurice Conly in 2005 from a photograph, using a conte pencil and chalk. *(RNZAF Wigram, MUS 050233)*

*Top:* Johnny doing what didn't come naturally: making a speech (apparently successfully) at Taieri, near Dunedin, in 1946, when he commanded that station. The word behind him is 'Haeremai', Maori for 'welcome'. *(RNZAF Central Photographic Establishment, G 11221, Box 254)*

*Middle:* The author with Johnny in the RSA Memorial Hall, Invercargill, where the first edition of this biography was launched, in his birthplace and on his 75th birthday, 20 February 1987. (Southland Times, *21 February 1987)*

*Bottom:* Moth Doctors. Seven men in white coats in a Wigram hangar, 25 June 1991. 'These were the best days of all my service', Johnny said. 'Doing just what I wanted to do when I felt like doing it.' Back row: Arch Beazer, Spencer Barnard, Johnny Checketts; front row: Jim Grant, Jim Williams, Bob Swadell, Vic Braggins.

*Top:* Johnny as tour guide at the RNZAF Museum, Wigram, Christchurch in 1994. He is standing behind one of that museum's many lifelike and well-dressed mannequins. (Christchurch Star)

*Bottom left:* Johnny, in helmet and goggles, testing a newly-acquired Spitfire simulator at Wigram in December 1995. Unpainted Hudson in the background. Flight Sergeant Bill McIndoe offers advice: 'he thought I might try to take off', Johnny laughed.

At Johnny's suggestion, the simulator carries Alan Deere's Kiwi device and the letters of a Spitfire he flew during the Battle of Britain. (MUS 960314)

*Bottom right:* Museum Guides. Six men in blazers at Wigram in front of a Skyhawk, 3 July 2000: Johnny was then 88 and, as he said, 'there was still some petrol left in the tank'. Back row: Colin Rudd, Charles Tapper, Colin Bailey; front row: Frank Blay, Johnny Checketts, Ted Burns. (MUS 000891)

JOHN MILNE CHECKETTS
(JOHNNY)
1912 - 2006

You can shed tears that he is gone
or you can smile because he has lived.

*Top:* Johnny at home on his 90th birthday, 20 February 2002. Among the pictures on the wall behind him is a print of his beloved Spitfire in flight and portraits of his friends Al Deere and Edward 'Hawkeye' Wells, another important influence on his career as a fighter pilot.

*Middle left:* Johnny's magnificent garden, at 16 Hudson Street, Christchurch, his home for the last 33 years of his life.

*Middle right:* Johnny celebrating that birthday in front of William Dring's portrait of him, made in September 1944.

*Left:* This photograph, cleverly made by family members, was used at Johnny's funeral  actually, a celebration of his life, as they preferred to think of it  in St. Matthew's Anglican Church, Christchurch, on 26 April 2006. Johnny always added a little biplane to his signature and here, for the last time, his son Christopher did the honours.

escape from death, he realised that he must soon go 'into the bag': without help — both medical and material — he could do nothing.

He then heard a low whistle behind him and spun round to see a peasant crouching nearby, beckoning him further into the wood. Johnny followed until they came to a hollow where the peasant signalled him to lie down. He did so and was covered thickly with leaves and earth and urged to keep quiet. Lying on his stomach, the hard ground and rough leaves irritated his burns until, mercifully, he lost consciousness. It was dark when he was awakened by a man lying beside him and whispering 'intelligence, intelligence' quietly in his ear. He lifted his head and the man pushed it firmly back into the leaves: 'Shush,' he said, 'Boche.' When the pressure on his head eased, Johnny carefully looked up. Only a few metres away he saw a German soldier standing very still, clearly outlined against the sky. Stiff, cold and aching from head to foot, he forced himself to lie still while the man gently swept the leaves from his back and legs. The man then tugged his arm, indicating that he should follow. They crept slowly and quietly out of the wood and into a muddy, evil-smelling ditch. They crawled along this ditch for hours, pausing only when Johnny was too exhausted to go on without a rest, until at last they were able to stand upright, climb out of the ditch and cross some fields leading to a farmhouse.

The man knocked lightly on the door, a woman opened it at once and they hurried in. She closed all the curtains, lit a candle and began to tend the wounds on Johnny's face brisky and efficiently, bathing it with warm water and potato juice. This treatment proved wonderfully soothing, but when he tried to drink a glass of apple wine a sharp pain told him that the inside of his mouth had been burned by the hot air sucked in through his oxygen mask after it caught fire. She smiled and gave him a lump of sugar instead. The man now reappeared with a bicycle and Johnny was placed on it, but his legs were so stiff and sore that he could not pedal and the man had to push him along. Further rest was impossible because the Germans knew exactly where he had landed and were already searching the area systematically; they would certainly reach that farmhouse within the next few hours. Thus began another long and painful journey, ending just at daybreak, when they arrived at the man's home seven kilometres from the village of Tours-en-Vimeu and fifteen kilometres from

Abbeville. His wife was waiting for them with a peasant who turned out to be a Typhoon pilot, Flying Officer Edwin (Ted) Aldridge Haddock of 181 Squadron, shot down seven weeks previously.

The man's name was Marcel Lecointe and his wife was called Charlotte. She cooked a meal of tomatoes and breadcrumbs and fed Johnny with a teaspoon. His mouth was very sore, but he had not enjoyed the taste of fresh tomatoes for such a long time that he willingly put up with the pain; he was, in any case, very hungry. Marcel and Charlotte then led him into a small room opening off the rear of the kitchen. Together they gently undressed him, ignoring his embarrassment, and laid him on a bed. Charlotte washed and dressed his wounds skilfully and then they covered him with a single sheet (he could bear nothing heavier) and left him to sleep.

Sleep, of course, was impossible: his mind was too full of fearful or unique experiences crammed into the last twelve hours to permit that blessed release, and his body ached in too many places. He knew that he would by now have been posted as missing. If Houlton had managed to get home safely his report could hardly be encouraging because the Spitfire had been going down in flames when he last saw it. Johnny's family and friends, not least Natalie, would hear no good news of him for the foreseeable future. But in fact the news Doug Brown heard and sent home only six days later was that 'he is a POW and badly injured: I sincerely hope he was not burned as I don't think the Huns are as efficient as our doctors in the patching up of burns.' Natalie was teaching in Waimate, South Canterbury, when she learned from Johnny's father that he was missing. As far as most New Zealanders knew, anyone who went missing became, at best, a prisoner. This was the news she had from Alan Deere, that the Germans had captured him. It was, of course, a wonderful comfort to believe that he might not be dead or even seriously wounded, but it never occurred to her that he might have evaded capture.

Meanwhile, on Johnny's first morning in France, a French doctor had already done his best for him by giving him an anti-tetanus injection. While he was still treating him, with Ted Haddock's assistance, there came a sudden violent hammering at the front door. The doctor and Ted disappeared smartly through the rear window before Charlotte opened the door to speak to a German soldier and Johnny suddenly realised that not only was he about to be captured but that his French friends would be in serious trouble. The soldier, however, did not search the house and about an hour later Ted (who understood French) returned to explain what had happened. There had actually been five soldiers at the front door, but they were not looking for airmen on the run; only butter. Charlotte had none, having used her last cooking for Johnny. The soldiers accepted her word and left, deciding not to look for themselves.

Johnny spent a wretched day, restless in mind and body alike. By mid-afternoon, he could not see at all because the burns on his face were so swollen, but Marcel and Charlotte tended him with loving care. Charlotte had a bottle of Mercurochrome, a red antiseptic, and painted his wounds every two hours until a skin formed over them (he still has the bottle). The swelling gradually went down and by the third day he could see again. There were several pieces of shrapnel in his right knee, but the doctor refused to risk a second visit and so Charlotte took them all out, using a sterilised kitchen fork. However, it was some time before he was able to walk, even with a stick. Far worse than all his pain was his fear of what would happen to these brave, kind people if the Germans raided the house and caught him. He explained this to them (through Ted) and they merely laughed, pointing to the loft. He was unconvinced; it seemed to him that the loft was an obvious hiding-place, but he said nothing more.

One morning, a whole column of German troops arrived outside the house, parked their vehicles and camouflaged them with nets and branches. Marcel had gone to work in the village (he was a hairdresser) and Ted helped Johnny into the loft before taking refuge himself in the fields behind the house. There were pieces of a Morane-Saulnier fighter in the loft, presumably souvenired by Marcel, and lots of apples. Peeping out through cracks in the tiles, he could see soldiers strolling about and hear their voices clearly. They stayed there all day, totally ignoring the house and those near it, before moving off at dusk. Marcel seemed quite unconcerned about the Germans. He would sit on his doorstep, scrounging cigarettes for Johnny from soldiers passing by, and took extraordinary risks to get whatever he wanted for his unexpected guests. The boy with the bicycle who had helped Johnny to the wood called one day to see him; so, too, did the village priest, bringing a bottle of wine. Johnny, now on the mend, was learning to communicate in sign language. Charlotte was a cheerful girl as well as a devoted nurse, and they shared some good laughs together. Marcel's mother, however, who lived next door, talked too much both inside and outside the house and took what seemed to Johnny an undue interest in his body, burned and unburned parts alike.

After a week in this house, Marcel brought a man to see him who said he was a member of the Resistance and his code name was 'the architect'. He questioned Johnny closely about his base and fellow pilots, but Johnny refused to answer. The architect replied that he needed the information for transmission to England; without it the Resistance might regard him as a spy and refuse to help him. Johnny still refused to answer. The Royal Air Force instructed all pilots unlucky enough to land in Occupied Territory to tell no-one, apparent friend or certain enemy, anything except number, rank and name. The man went away, muttering crossly. Nevertheless, he turned up a couple of days later with a bundle of typical peasant clothes. Some items were too large, others too small, but Johnny was grateful for everything; he was literally helpless without them and tried hard to show his gratitude to the architect who still seemed annoyed with him.

Two weeks of anxiety and discomfort slowly passed away. But his wounds were healing, his strength returning and he was well enough to enjoy a small party to celebrate Marcel's twenty-sixth birthday. They feasted off rabbit, marvellously cooked with a host of delicious vegetables, washed down with wine, brandy and liqueurs, all carefully saved for the occasion. Even at the time, in the middle of an apparently endless war and worried as he was about his family and Natalie and his chances of getting back into action again, it seemed a thoroughly *happy* evening; looking back on it at intervals over the next forty-odd years, it has never lost its peculiar intensity: 'It was such a hard time for all of us, and I suppose we simply felt the need to have some fun when we could; we were young still and glad to be alive.'

The architect called to say that a Lysander aircraft would turn up one night soon to drop agents and carry him back to England, but a day or two later he called again to say that the Germans had found out about the proposed drop and the venture was off. Although disappointed, Johnny refused to despair. He learned from an old man who used to fill in bomb craters at Poix aerodrome (about thirty kilometres to the south) that two Fw 190 fighters had been left there under the guard of a few soldiers when the rest of the unit moved to Holland. Having already flown that type, he felt certain that he could get home in one of them. He was quite prepared to run the risks involved: to be caught breaking curfew meant being handed over to the dreaded Gestapo, who would soon establish his true identity (and, incidentally, that of the men and women who had befriended him); should he escape capture, he would still have to avoid the mines and cut the barbed wire guarding the airfield; he would then have to deal with at least one fit, armed German sentry although he was at that time unfit, unarmed and hobbling about with a stick; should he succeed in taking off in an unchecked aircraft, he would learn only after takeoff whether it carried enough fuel to cross the Channel; and during that flight he would certainly be picked up by British radar and very likely shot down by British fighters or coastal batteries. At first, the old man was eager to take him to Poix, but fortunately for all concerned he had second thoughts. Johnny fumed and fretted until he learned that both aircraft were unserviceable (the obvious reason for leaving them behind) but his plan had never been sensible.

It was frustrating to be so close to England and yet unable to get there. As Johnny said: 'I now began to understand how the Germans had felt for the last three years; very tantalising!' His sense of frustration was heightened every fine day by the sight of British fighters and bombers either cruising out to their targets in well-ordered formations or fleeing home in twos and threes. He knew exactly what they were hoping and fearing and flew with them, in imagination, as long as he could see or hear anything. At times, he even fancied that he could pick out Biggin Hill's Spitfires and named the pilots of the tiny dots racing far overhead. He and Ted Haddock spent hours talking somewhat despondently about their prospects of returning to England. Ted had now been in France for more than two months and both men naturally supposed that if and when the Resistance did arrange anything, then he would be the first to go; Johnny would have to wait his turn. In fact, Ted's flying days were over. He was captured a few weeks later and spent the rest of the war in a German prison camp.

Marcel came home one evening to say that Johnny was to be moved next morning. Having said farewell to Charlotte, trying vainly to express his gratitude and his earnest desire to return one day and thank her properly for her tender care, he and Marcel walked a little way out of the village at about 7 a.m. until they were picked up by a tiny Citroën Cloverleaf, powered by a charcoal burner which smoked furiously. Marcel sat beside the driver and Johnny jammed himself into 'an absence of space' between and behind them. They drove towards Abbeville until they reached a World War I cemetery where he was told to get out and hide. The Citroën chugged noisily away, leaving him skulking among the tombstones of men who had so recently fought a war to end all wars and now the sons of those men were fighting the same war over the same country yet again. 'I didn't often let things get me down,' he recalled, 'but they did that morning: looking at all those graves of chaps younger than me on such a beautiful, peaceful morning with birds singing everywhere, the war seemed such a bloody waste of time and I felt so alone and helpless; I got really fed up. However, I had to make the best of it.'

After about an hour and a half, the Citroën chugged back — 'but without my dear friend Marcel' and without any explanation of his absence. Johnny was again bundled into the space behind the front seats and Marcel's place was now occupied by a man he had not met. It soon became clear that he was well-known to the Germans and had come along in order to make cheerful conversation whenever necessary; the driver (a blacksmith in Abbeville) was also able to gossip easily with them. As for Johnny, he was told to cover his scarred face with a handkerchief and act dumb: 'That was easy enough, I *was* dumb; I was also terrified.' The Citroën crossed the Somme and trundled along the road to Hesdin, passing right alongside the airfield at Abbeville. Johnny saw German fighters at dispersal and their pilots lolling in the shade on that lovely morning, looking just like his comrades at Biggin Hill.

Eventually, they reached a small but imposing château. He was told to get out, the car was immediately driven away and Johnny was left standing before the front door looking at an elderly lady. She calmly informed him, in quite good English, that although the ground floor of the château was used to accommodate German NCOs manning a nearby flak battery, he would be perfectly safe in the attic. He was there for three days, listening to the Germans roistering down below at night time and scarcely daring to move. During the days, the lady talked to him about her family (she traced her family back over three centuries to Scotland) and her service as a nurse in World War I; he told her about his Scottish-Irish descent and his home in Invercargill. He thought her 'a lovely person' with a dry sense of humour that he liked very much. For example, she dressed his burns and manipulated the sores to make them look syphilitic and so discourage the Germans from examining him too closely. She gave him an English Bible, a gift which he greatly treasured. Many years later, he would give it to his daughter.

Johnny was moved from there to Auxi-le-Château (an important road junction on the Authie river which reaches the sea a little north of the Somme Estuary) in another, larger Citroën by an English-speaking driver. There were many military vehicles on the road and Johnny was becoming more and more afraid of capture because by now, with his wounds dressed and healing, it would be obvious to the Germans that he had received assistance and he dreaded to think what he might say under torture. He had no identity papers, ration tickets or work permits and even the simplest questioning would instantly reveal that he was not French. Moreover, he felt distinctly uneasy about his latest driver: a Typhoon pilot, so he claimed, who had been shot down some six months previously and decided to remain in France to assist the Resistance because he spoke French, German and English fluently. He said that he worked for the Germans as a driver and that the Citroën actually belonged to them, a fact which he found vastly amusing. He was courteous and competent, but Johnny did not trust him: he talked too much about himself and his work to a perfect stranger.

No disaster occurred, however, and they arrived safely at the home of a French policeman. Johnny there met four other would-be escapers. One was a Norwegian pilot, known as Libby, who had been shot down some five months earlier. Libby was a big, blond man and — as Johnny later learned — 'very uncouth'. Two were survivors from a crashed Boston bomber and the fourth a sturdy chap with a shaggy moustache, wearing a beret and carrying a small parcel under his arm. There were also three or four Frenchmen and altogether too much noisy conversation for his peace of mind, which was further disturbed when he learned that the escapers were to be sent on a journey of over 500 kilometres westward to Douarnenez, near Brest, where a British submarine would call for them. He stood by himself, glowering at the floor for some time before he noticed that the chap with the moustache was also standing alone and looking as uncomfortable as he felt. 'Are you English?' he asked. The man mumbled in French, but Johnny guessed he was English. 'My name is Johnny Checketts,' he announced. There was a short silence and then the man said: 'Well, Sir, you're my C.O. I'm Terry Kearins.'

## CHAPTER NINE

# An Absorbing Manhunt (2): October 1943

Johnny had last seen Terry Kearins on 15 July, going down in flames at low altitude after an attack on Poix airfield; he saw no parachute and therefore reported him believed killed in action. His thoughts flew instantly to Terry's family in Palmerston North and to his English fiancée, whose grief might soon be changed to joy. Soon they were chattering away as eagerly as the rest of the men in the room. Like Johnny, Terry had baled out just in time and already owed his life and liberty to the French. Badly bruised and burned, he made his way (helped by several field labourers) from a point some seven kilometres west of Hesdin to an isolated farmhouse near Quesnoy-en-Artois, where he arrived exhausted and spent the next six weeks in bed, devotedly cared for by the farmer and his wife. Talking to Terry cleared Johnny's black mood and he was further cheered on learning that they would not, after all, be taken to Brest. Instead, they were to go to Amiens next morning and then by train to Paris.

The New Zealanders and Libby travelled in the Citroën with a new driver who boldly took the main road despite Johnny's protests. He then contrived to draw further attention to himself by taking a wrong turning at Canaples and having to stop and ask the way. Although there was plenty of German traffic on the road (Johnny wryly asked Terry why the Royal Air Force was not

shooting it up), it was French policemen who first stopped them
— and then quickly waved them on. Just outside Amiens, they
were stopped again: this time by Germans. A simple, routine request to show papers, even a casual remark that required an answer,
and they were done for. The driver gabbled away furiously to one
German while the others stood by, looking straight at three British
airmen. 'I sat there,' Johnny remembered. 'trying to bury my face
in the handkerchief and trembling with fear.' A lifetime later, so
it seemed, they were waved on. The driver took them to the station, bought them tickets to Paris and drove off: 'He'd lost his
bounce by then and couldn't get away quick enough.

The train was not due to leave for nearly an hour and they
agreed that they would be too conspicuous standing so long on
the platform. There was nothing for it but to wander through the
streets of the town, even though they were full of German soldiers.
Though Terry's French was good, Libby spoke fluent German
and could have provided the New Zealanders with excellent cover,
but he wandered off on his own and Johnny let him go. He always
felt uneasy in his company and was glad to see the back of him.
They had been given the description of a young woman who would
travel with them to Paris and lead them to a safe place when they
got there. They were to catch her eye before the train departed,
but not to speak to her nor travel in the same compartment. In
Paris, they were to follow her — not too closely — out of the station. Should the Germans question them en route, they must not
look to her for help; there would be nothing she could do. With
these bleak instructions ringing in his ears, Johnny braced himself
to endure the journey as best he could. Not only were there
numerous German soldiers and airmen aboard, but he had very
much in mind the appearance of the Amiens-Paris railway line
which he had last seen from behind the windscreen of a Spitfire.
It would be ironic, he thought, to be blasted to Kingdom Come
by one of his Biggin Hill mates.

The train stopped every few minutes, picking up more
passengers, and quickly became very crowded. At one station, the
compartment in which Johnny was travelling stopped beyond the
platform and intending passengers stood at track level, well below
the door sill. When the door was flung open, he saw the head
and shoulders of an old woman. She threw a large bag of vegetables

up on to the floor and then another bag in which were two live ducks, quacking furiously, their heads sticking out of holes. She caught his eye and fired a volley of words at him. He waved his arms about, desperately trying to indicate that he was deaf and dumb, until he realised that she only wanted him to haul her on board. As he did so, the other occupants of the compartment (all French at that time, except for Terry and Libby) began to mutter and some looked crossly at him. The compartment was already full enough, they thought, without the old woman and her noisy ducks. Like all fugitives, he wanted nothing more than to be total-ly ignored by those around him, but now he was the centre of attention. The old woman made matters worse: she gave him an apple and began to talk to him loudly. Fortunately, his mumbles and smiles were all the co-operation she needed. While the train was standing in the station at Le Bourget, he had more bad moments when some bemedalled Luftwaffe officers strolled non-chalantly through the compartment, looking for empty seats. They were perfectly capable, he thought, of asking to see his papers as an excuse to get him out of his seat.

At last the train reached its terminus, the Gare du Nord. Johnny spotted his guide and followed her, at a discreet distance, with Terry and Libby. Their tickets were accepted without fuss, but outside the station three German soldiers were making a random check of papers. He realised that it would be fatal to turn back into the station and guessed that the soldiers would be looking particularly for persons who hesitated or tried to give them a wide berth. Taking a deep breath, he marched boldly towards the nearest guard, kept his head up and passed by as close as possible; Terry and Libby followed and none of them were stopped. This was the first time he had tried to walk more than a few metres since being shot down and soon he was limping badly. Although both legs were stiff and sore, his left foot (containing a piece of shrapnel that Charlotte had been unable to get out) caused most trouble. It began to bleed and the wounds on his face were now throbbing painfully. He felt exhausted, but Terry helped to keep him going.

Following their guide, they went down to the Metro and travelled underground, using tickets given them in Amiens. It was the rush hour and the compartment was so full that they often lost sight of their guide amongst a sea of bodies, all pushing and shoving;

Johnny by now was so weak that he needed Terry's support. Eventually they caught her signal to struggle out and Johnny managed to walk steadily through the ticket-barrier and past the guards at the station exit. They made their way in the dark through a maze of narrow alleys in the Pont de Versailles district and into a tall building with an ancient lift which took them to the top floor. There they found themselves in a large room full of Allied airmen, about twenty of them, mostly American survivors of crashed heavy bombers.

They were warmly welcomed and someone produced soup. They pooled the food parcels they had carried from Amiens (bread, cheese, potatoes) and even enjoyed a glass of brandy. That night they did not realise how scarce food and drink were in Paris, but they learned quickly enough next day when they had to boil the potato peelings with whatever scraps they could find. They remained in that building for two or three days (sleeping as best they could on the floor without mattresses or blankets, trying not to think about either food or the Gestapo) while papers were forged for them. Johnny was made a bus driver with papers suitably endorsed to show that he was currently too ill to work. He thought them beautiful papers, convincingly grubby and tattered, and was relieved to possess at last something that he could show the Germans.

As soon as everyone had papers, the underground organisers dispersed the airmen. Johnny, Terry and Libby were put on a train for Sens, about a hundred kilometres south-east of Paris, en route for Switzerland. Johnny was now so used to the sight and sound of German soldiers that he 'began to feel a wee bit of confidence that if we didn't do anything stupid, they would simply ignore us. The Gestapo, however, were quite a different matter.' He had heard terrifying stories about their brutality and cunning since landing in France; they would not be fooled by his forged papers, he thought, and even if they were, the burns still clearly visible on his face would reveal him as an airman. They were renowned for snap checks on trains to check travellers' documents and he was in an agony of apprehension throughout the very slow journey to Sens. There they found the local people unwilling to take them in because some locomotives had been destroyed by saboteurs the night before. The Germans were making house-to-house searches and would certainly interrogate very carefully any strangers they caught. It was therefore decided that the New Zealanders should go on to Joigny, about thirty kilometres farther south: a car took them part of the way, but they had to walk the rest and Johnny caught a cold to add to his other troubles. At least they were rid of Libby. He stayed in Sens and Johnny hoped they might never see him again.

At Joigny, two old ladies — Gabrielle and Louise Meyer — took them in, gave them turnip soup and bread and hid them in an attic with a single tiny bed. It was too small for both of them and Johnny told Terry to have it for the first night. During that night, however, his cold worsened into a severe bout of influenza and Terry insisted that he have the bed for the rest of their time there, though he was none too fit himself. The old ladies took turns to cycle into the country each morning, seeking vegetables with which to make soup for their guests, but food was almost as scarce in Joigny as in Paris and often it was late afternoon before Gabrielle or Louise returned, not heavily laden.

The New Zealanders could see into the street from the attic window and Johnny was looking out one afternoon when he saw Louise pedalling slowly down the street, balancing a large parcel of vegetables on her crossbar. Meanwhile, a squad of young German soldiers was marching up the street, singing lustily, on their way to a cinema. Louise dismounted, waiting for them to pass. She was not in their way, but one of the soldiers chose to put his shoulder into her; she fell over her bicycle, the parcel came undone and turnips, parsnips and carrots scattered over the footpath. The soldier laughed, so did his comrades, and they all carried on into the cinema, still singing cheerfully. Johnny had rarely been angry with the Germans before this incident, even while in deadly combat with them, but this act of casual contempt brought home to him, more even than the many stories of calculated brutality which he had heard, what the French were suffering — day after day — at the hands of their conquerors. Since landing in France, he had usually been too ill or frightened to feel much anger; from now on, however, anger would help to sustain him until he returned to England.

That night, a young Frenchman visited the New Zealanders. He had sunk two barges, blown up a train and wanted to store his remaining explosives in the attic, but the old ladies refused to entertain the idea. He clearly terrified them and Johnny could see why: German reaction to acts of sabotage was so violent and indiscriminate that the harm done to them never outweighed the suffering they inflicted. On the other hand, he sympathised with the young man and those like him who were unable to endure their subjection. A few days later, Johnny and Terry had a more welcome visitor: a man who came from Paris to say that the old plan of returning to England by submarine from Douarnenez had been revived and they were not to continue their journey to Switzerland.

Johnny would receive two or three letters from Gabrielle after the war, but Louise died in May 1945. 'The bells of victory were ringing,' wrote Gabrielle, 'when she left home and that victory we had eagerly awaited for so long remains now in my heart darkened with sorrow.' Do you remember your stay, she asked in one letter, 'in that small house and your tiny room lacking of comfort, but so well hidden and far from the watching of any creatures — the Boches especially? . . . We were so happy, my sister and I, to receive and protect so valiant and brave men as you [and Terry] are!'

The New Zealanders returned to Paris via Sens, where (much to Johnny's disgust) Libby rejoined them, together with the noisiest American he ever met. 'He was a very nice fellow,' Johnny recalls, 'but he couldn't even walk along the street without drawing attention to himself, talking or coughing loudly and banging into things and people; he was a holy terror to be with.' From their old room in Paris, they travelled by train to Vannes in Brittany, via Orléans, Tours and Nantes, a journey of some 530 kilometres. They left in the evening, travelled all night and arrived in Nantes early next morning. As usual, the train was full of Germans as well as French civilians and, as usual, the fugitives were in constant fear of the Gestapo. Johnny once again attracted the attention of a French woman and this time was given *two* apples. He realised that quite a few of his fellow passengers, on this as on his other journeys, had penetrated his flimsy disguise, but no-one betrayed him even though the Germans were offering generous rewards for information leading to the capture of Allied airmen.

The three fugitives were billeted by a family named Levanant at their farm outside Vannes. Although their living conditions were primitive, the people were so warm-hearted that Johnny soon felt completely at home. There was a long, narrow kitchen dominated by a huge open fireplace where most of the cooking was done on an iron ring, though there was a small oven beside it. At one side, the kitchen opened into a bedroom just large enough for the farmer and his wife; at the other, it opened into a room for cattle, pigs and poultry. Above the kitchen was a hayloft and places for three children (and visiting airmen) to sleep. The farmer, though deaf and dumb, was very shrewd and hard-working; his wife was short and plump with a lovely face, in Johnny's eyes, and a cheerful smile. Both were very active in the Resistance and their eldest daughter, Marie, would be awarded the Legion of Honour after the war for her outstanding courage and resolution. The farm was so isolated that at first sight it seemed an ideal refuge, but Johnny soon learned that German soldiers and sailors were thick on the ground in that region. Vannes formed part of the much-vaunted 'Atlantic Wall'; Lorient, a submarine station, lay only forty kilometres to the north and power lines leading to the great naval base at Brest (a further 110 kilometres north) provided a tempting target for saboteurs and were therefore constantly patrolled by soldiers with dogs.

Their guide from Vannes to the farm was a most attractive young woman, Agnès de la Barre de Nanteuil, who brought bread and vegetables for the airmen every second day. She used to arrive early in the morning, scruffily dressed, her face dirty and her hair in a tangle, to avoid the attentions of predatory Germans. For the same reason, she stayed at the farm until late afternoon, leaving just in time to get home before curfew. Johnny therefore had time to get to know her and they became close friends. After a week they left the farm and spent a night in Vannes at Agnès home. She gave him a small piece of paper (still in his possession) on which she had written out in English the three verses of Cardinal Newman's great hymn so relevant to Johnny's dangerous situation:

Lead kindly light, amid the encircling gloom,
Lead Thou me on!
The night is dark and I am far from home
Lead Thou me on!
Keep Thou my feet: I do not ask to see
The distant scene; one step enough for me.

Agnes wrote above these words 'The Pillar of the Cloud', a reference to Exodus, chapter 13, verses 21 and 22, in which the Lord guided the Israelites through the wilderness: 'There never failed the pillar of the cloud by day, nor the pillar of fire by night, before the people.'

Next morning, the fugitives travelled by train to Quimper through a military zone 'absolutely teeming with German soldiers and sailors'. It was a very slow journey, strictly policed by armed guards, because wrecked locomotives, carriages and waggons lay alongside the track in many places. Some had been destroyed by the Allied Air Forces, but most were the victims of local saboteurs. Johnny sensed a much sharper hostility between the French and their rulers during this stage of his journey along the vulnerable frontier of Fortress Europe than he had experienced hitherto. Here, he suspected, the Germans might well execute a captured airman on the spot.

He and Terry left the train at a village before reaching Quimper in order to break their trail because German guards at that sensitive base were apt to scrutinise particularly carefully the papers of young men arriving from Vannes, where there was a direct link with Paris, and with other young men who were, by this time, almost openly rebellious. Consequently, they hid in the cold damp vestry of a church, without food or drink, for the rest of that day and the next. There they were joined by other fugitives, among them a Frenchman wanted by the Germans for forced labour. Johnny was now so tired and weak that he would willingly have slept, but his loud snores forced his companions to shake him awake whenever he nodded off. A door led from the vestry into the church and at one time they heard someone moving about in there. Everyone froze while the intruder approached the door and tried to open it. The Frenchman drew a knife and stood just inside the door. Johnny felt certain that he was ready to kill whoever opened that door, but it was locked and after trying it for some time the intruder went away.

Eventually a guide came to lead them along a winding track to another village where they boarded a small local train and arrived in Quimper exhausted, not needing to pretend to be weary, bedraggled peasants incapable of posing any threat to Fortress Europe; their manner was perfect and the station guards hardly glanced at them. The New Zealanders had been told to meet their next guide on a particular street corner in Quimper. When she failed to appear, they kept their heads and walked purposefully round the town, sticking close to other pedestrians. By now, they were well aware of the danger of hanging about alone in public places. After fifteen minutes, they returned to the meeting place and were greatly relieved to find a woman waiting for them. She took them to a café where they were given soup and bread (their first meal of the day) and then shown upstairs to a room with a huge double bed and a lovely soft mattress. There was ample room for both of them and despite their fears they were soon fast asleep.

During the night, they were suddenly awakened by noises from below. Soldiers were pounding on the outside door and their host was racing up the stairs to warn the fugitives and make the bed almost before they were out of it. They scrambled hastily for their clothes. Terry disappeared down the stairs and Johnny followed. He had one leg in his trousers, one boot on and the rest of his clothes in his arms. The Germans were still hammering at the door and loudly demanding admittance; their host's wife was screaming her head off but making no effort to unbar the door; their host, having now straightened the bed, was yelling down the stairs. Johnny found himself in a kitchen, groping blindly in pitch blackness for a rear exit, the noises he made being covered by the screams and yells of the café owner and his wife.

He stumbled out of the house, across a yard, through a gate and into a hen run. The birds fluttered about, squawking furiously, but he had no time to seek a better hiding place and so he crouched down in the straw beside their perches. He forced himself to sit still and willed the birds to settle. Lights came on in the house, he heard the front door open and the sound of angry German voices, submissive French voices. 'I have never been so frightened,' he remembers. 'I took it for granted that the Germans would search the place and find me, but what really petrified me was the thought that they would shoot me there and then, in among the hens.' The voices died away. No-one came into the yard, but Johnny did not dare to move even though he still had only one leg in his trousers and one boot on. The hens, not surprisingly, were outraged by his presence and glared at him so indignantly that any further disturbance would, he thought, cause them to set up such an uproar as would summon half the German army. He therefore stayed perfectly still, trying to look like a hen's best friend.

The night slowly wore away until at last he heard someone come into the yard carrying a candle and calling 'Johnny, Johnny', very softly. It was his host, the café owner. He and his wife were most amused to see him covered in dung and half-dressed; once he had a cup of hot coffee in his hands and a warm blanket round his shoulders, Johnny also began to see the funny side of the night's events. As for Terry, he had found his way into the middle of a cabbage patch and lain there, like Johnny, frightened and frozen stiff. They learned that their visitors had in fact been the Gestapo, looking for a house with that number but in a different street. Such mistakes were not uncommon and the Gestapo usually carried out a vigorous search anyway in the well-found belief that something or someone of interest would be turned up. This time, however, they were in a hurry and merely threatened the café-owner and his wife with arrest if they did not open their door promptly in future. As soon as daylight came, many men and women called to meet the fugitives and hear at first hand what had happened during the night. Although their friendliness was encouraging, it alarmed the New Zealanders to learn how many people knew about them. They tried to hide their anxiety, but in fact they were greatly relieved to leave Quimper that afternoon. 'I guess we just weren't as brave as they were,' said Johnny.

More than five years later, in December 1948, Fernand Nargeot (the son of Johnny's hosts) wrote to him from Paris. Fernand had recently visited London and while walking past New Zealand House suddenly remembered that alarming night. 'We were all sleeping or almost all,' he wrote, 'when at four o'clock in the night the Gestapo knocked the door. Do you remember how we startled you out of bed and the rush in the garden? I'll never forget. The poor lady who brought you to our place was arrested a few weeks later and deported in Germany. She came back to France after the liberation but she died after a year. She was somebody.'

From Quimper, Johnny and Terry went to Crozon, a small fishing village, where they were hidden with two American pilots in a house next door to the Hotel Saint de Marine. Their host actually owned the hotel, but the Luftwaffe had ejected him and turned it into a Mess for officers serving with a nearby recon-naissance and anti-shipping unit. During the next few days, Johnny watched Ju 88s and Fw 190s taking off and landing; he played chess and cards; most of all, he worried about his host who was frequently indiscreet and sometimes stupidly rude to the Germans. He was glad to leave Crozon and learned later that the Gestapo had arrested their host not two hours after their departure and ransacked his house.

On they travelled, tense and weary, their hopes of escape at times almost overwhelmed by fears of capture, torture and betrayal until they reached another fishing village — Camaret, in Brest harbour — where they were hidden in a bakery and told they would soon be boarding a fishing vessel bound for England. Twenty-six Allied airmen — men whom Johnny first met in Paris — reached that bakery. In twos and threes they had followed much the same route as he and Terry and so far not one had been caught. The last lap, however, was likely to prove the most dangerous. The Germans kept a careful watch on the road leading along the water's edge and on boats rowing out to fishing vessels anchored in the stream. The fugitives would have to make their own way singly or in pairs from the bakery down to a particular dinghy without being seen by foot patrols. When two or three were aboard, they would be rowed out to the *Suzette* (a ten metre lobster boat) an-chored about twenty metres off shore; choosing a safe moment, they would scramble aboard from the seaward side. The dinghy would return to the water's edge and pick up two or three more men. Johnny and Terry successfully reached the launch, but when thirteen airmen were aboard the fishermen decided they could risk no more trips and the launch could carry no more passengers. Johnny never learned what became of the thirteen men still hiding in the bakery.

The movements of fishing vessels were severely restricted. Very little fuel was made available; they were not permitted to stay at sea for longer than twenty-four hours; if a boat disappeared the rest of the fleet was forbidden to sail for two months and, not least, German aircraft and patrol boats kept a close watch on them. Consequently, not many fishermen were prepared to run the grave risks involved in carrying fugitives across the Channel. The crew of the *Suzette* nevertheless agreed to run the gauntlet. But for five days bad weather prevented her putting to sea.

The thirteen 'lucky' airmen spent those days crammed below the tiny *Suzette*'s deck, sharing a single lavatory bucket that could only be emptied at nightfall. They crouched along the vessel's sides, huddling together for a little warmth, and took turns to occupy a small evil-smelling cabin where two men could sit on a bench, almost upright, and two could stretch out in narrow bunks. Only at night were they able to stand upright, in the hold or engine well, and breathe fresh air. At all times they had to move cautiously and speak only in whispers, acutely conscious of the Germans patrolling the harbour road only a few metres away. They had very little to eat or drink, their spirits were low and several tempers frayed under the strain. Bitter words were exchanged and once or twice men scuffled with each other despite all that Johnny (as the senior officer aboard) could say or do. On the third day, the fishermen brought them some hard bread, a can of water, a small piece of pork and a bottle of brandy. The water was contaminated with diesel oil and all who drank it became violently sick; the pork was far from fresh, but each man got so little that it did no harm; as for the brandy, two men gulped most of it as it was being passed around and Johnny only just prevented an outbreak of open fighting.

Early on the sixth morning, Johnny bet Terry three pounds that they would never get away. No sooner had he done so than the fishermen came on board and announced that the whole fleet would sail at 9 a.m. The *Suzette* moved out to the harbour boom and two German sailors came aboard. Jammed into the hold, the airmen heard them tramping about in the tiny cabin. One sailor wanted to inspect the hold, but ropes and lobsterpots lay over the cover; the weather was worsening again and he decided not to bother. Even when the boat cleared the harbour the airmen had to remain below, out of sight of German flak posts and fishermen in other boats. The fleet sailed south-westward in moderate seas and set lobster pots. The *Suzette* was allowed to drift away from the rest of the fleet and as soon as darkness fell the engine was started and a course set for Penzance in Cornwall. At last the airmen were able to come up on deck. A stiff cold breeze and thoughts of England briefly revived them, but they were too sea-sick to enjoy their liberty. By daybreak, even the sight of German air-craft on the southern horizon did not trouble them. In mid-afternoon, a British destroyer racing in from the Atlantic passed them without a sign, but a little later two Typhoons appeared and escorted them to a rendezvous with a naval launch which led them into Penzance.

There was a scramble to get ashore and Johnny was glad to see the back of all his travelling companions except Terry. The *Suzette* carried a large square tub of wine and he decided to sample a glass before going ashore. He had been too sea-sick to try it earlier and welcomed this chance of a few minutes alone — and without fear — for the first time in seven weeks. He felt also a need to pay quiet tribute to those brave men and women, perfect strangers whose language he could not speak, who made it possi-ble for him to avoid (at best) a prison camp and gave him a chance to get back into the fight and help bring their subjection to an end. All too soon the Flag Lieutenant of the Port Admiral was helping him ashore, introducing him to the Admiral and leading him into a dining-room where he sat down with his fellow refugees to a feed of brown bread, margarine and spam. After the meal, they were driven to an American camp where they shed their filthy clothes and dived into a hot bath. Johnny had not seen such dirty water around him since his rugby-playing days and had never used so much soap on himself, but it felt wonderful to be clean again.

They were issued with warm, comfortable clothes (American khaki fatigue drill) and then a British military policeman arrived to spoil their happy mood. They were under open arrest, he said, pending investigation of their stories; they would be taken at once to Falmouth and from there by train to London and would not be allowed to communicate with anyone until further notice. Johnny, however, refused to allow the policeman to spoil his con-tentment. Even though he was as weak as a kitten, having lost two stone in weight from his already slim frame, he felt clean and comfortable, neither hungry nor thirsty. His various burns and wounds would shortly receive expert attention; he would soon be able to sleep all night long in his own bed, with sheets and blankets; he had the lovely English countryside to gaze upon and — best of all — no fear that at any moment the Gestapo would appear and subject him to such torture that he might betray those who had helped him. At Paddington station a young second lieutenant in the United States Army mistook them for a bunch of newly-arrived American soldiers and attempted to march them smartly off the platform. Johnny swiftly disabused him, much to the amusement of his fellow escapees, and for a moment they all felt a sense of fellowship greater than any they ever had while on the run in France. From Paddington, he was taken to the Great Central Hotel at Marylebone railway station by representatives of MI 9.

MI 9, together with its American counterpart (MIS-X, from 1942 onwards), encouraged escape and evasion throughout Occupied Europe. Neither organisation had many trained agents in the field and both depended on several thousand volunteers to contact men — mostly airmen before D-Day — and hide them until they could be brought to safety. 'Initially, and very naturally,' wrote Lieutenant-Colonel J. M. Langley, the officer responsible for escape and evasion from France, Belgium and Holland, 'the Royal Air Force were sceptical as to the practical value of lectures on escape and evasion, the issue of "escape packs", foreign currency, compasses and maps: but when the end product walked into the mess with a cheery "Well chaps, I'm back", everything changed.' Airmen were naturally delighted to see lost friends restored and to realise that they themselves might well be as lucky, should they survive an unintentional landing across the Channel. Service authorities gradually became anxious to foster evasion (as opposed to escape) for these reasons and also because successful evaders were usually fitter than escapers; their skills and experience more recent and hence more valuable.

More than 3,000 Allied airmen evaded capture and returned to England before D-Day, but only about 300 of those did so from France, Belgium or Holland; the rest escaped via Spain. Their helpers paid a high price: over 500 civilians in those countries were killed by the Germans and many more were so weakened by torture or ill-treatment in concentration camps that they died prematurely after the war. 'For every successful evader,' wrote Jimmy Langley, 'a Belgian, Dutch or French helper gave his or her life.'

At the Great Central Hotel (where MI 9 had an interrogation centre), Johnny was subjected to detailed questioning by Langley, who had himself escaped from captivity in France despite losing an arm at Dunkirk. 'A handsome chap, beautifully-spoken', he nevertheless irritated Johnny by asking the same questions repeatedly and appearing not to believe the answers. As the interrogation dragged on, it seemed that Langley regarded him as a fool, a liar, even as a German spy. 'I became very angry indeed and said a few things in the heat of the moment that I shouldn't have.' Langley, however, remained perfectly calm and eventually Johnny was dismissed. Later that evening, as he sat alone at dinner, still brooding and fuming, Langley suddenly appeared. Smiling now, he told Johnny that he believed his story and, incidentally, admired the courage and determination he had shown throughout a very unpleasant time in France. But it was necessary, he went on, to test every story to destruction, if that were possible. Not every refugee was genuine and it was his job to identify the fakes. One effective test, he had found, was to make the refugee angry. The fake either stayed calm where an honest man would explode or pretended to be angry — and false anger, said Langley, was easy to detect. Moreover, the stimulus of anger made an honest man blurt out valuable details that might otherwise be forgotten. Johnny, relieved and embarrassed at the same time, had a couple of beers with Langley and decided that he was a real gentleman as well as 'a very hard case indeed' who would make any fakes he caught feel very sorry for themselves.

Johnny was given permission to telephone Air Vice-Marshal Hugh Saunders, head of 11 Group in Fighter Command, who, of course, was delighted to hear that he was back in England. His squadron, now commanded by Marty Hume, was at Hornchurch in Essex and Saunders promised to pass on the good news. An hour later, the Hornchurch wing leader — his old friend Bill Crawford-Compton — arrived at the interrogation centre. They were delighted to see each other and Bill swept him away to a favourite pub in Shepherd's Lane where many 485 Squadron pilots were waiting to welcome him. 'We were beginning to give up hope about Checks,' wrote Doug Brown, 'but you can't lose him that easily.' Although it was a joyous reunion, Johnny realised how much his grim experiences during the last seven weeks had weakened him when he struggled to down two pints and even had to ask Bill to take him home before the pub closed.

After a good breakfast of kippers, toast and marmalade, Johnny set off alone next morning for the Air Ministry, still wearing his American clothes. He was strolling along, looking for a taxi, when a jeep full of American military policemen pulled up and a very large sergeant, brandishing a truncheon, persuaded him to get in. Taking him for a thief or deserter and ignoring his protests, the Americans drove him to their depot where an officer listened stonily to his explanation, but finally agreed to ring the interrogation centre. Once his story had been confirmed, the jeep took him to the Air Ministry, hurtling through the London streets with scant regard for other road users. There he met a charming Air Commodore. Over excellent coffee and a couple of large whiskies, they discussed everything he could remember of military value: the location and extent of airfields and their defences, the number and type of aircraft and their ground dispersal, troop concentrations and their equipment, routes suitable for heavy transport, the amount of sabotage he had seen and the degree of tension he had noticed between the French and Germans on the Breton coast.

That evening, Johnny arrived at Hornchurch to find — as after his dip in the Channel eighteen months earlier — that most of his possessions had been dispersed among his comrades. Hugh Tucker returned his jacket, now bearing only the thin ring of a Pilot Officer, and someone found him a pair of trousers so that for the first time in nearly two months he looked like an honest airman again. Hugh Saunders visited Hornchurch next day to congratulate him on his escape and hear his story at first hand. They had lunch together and then the Air Vice-Marshal asked him what he would now like to do. More in hope than expectation he replied: 'Go back on operations, Sir.' Saunders smiled. 'No, that won't be possible for some time. You're not fit for that sort of pressure at the moment, but we'll find you an important job. It won't be flying a desk,' he added, as Johnny began to protest, 'I promise you that. And then? Well, we'll just have to see what next year brings.'

Thus Johnny lost his first squadron command and his place in the front line, but he knew that Saunders was right to rest him; indeed, it was a mark of considerable favour that so senior an officer should take the trouble to tell him personally and let him down gently. The news that he had escaped and was safe in England reached New Zealand too late to prevent Natalie's twenty-first birthday from being a sad, quiet affair, but with it came his request that she announce their engagement. 'Yes', she replied, by telegram. The postmaster told her she could have another twenty-three words for the same charge. 'Send it like that,' she said, 'I don't want to seem too eager.'

## CHAPTER TEN

# Teaching and Leading: November 1943 to September 1944

Johnny's good friend Alan Deere had just taken command of the fighter wing of Central Gunnery School at Sutton Bridge, following in the footsteps of Sailor Malan (who started the school), Jamie Rankin and Johnny Walker, his immediate predecessor. To his great joy, Johnny was sent there in November 1943 to command the Air-to-Air Combat Squadron: given that he was to be off operations for some months, no other posting could have pleased him so much. But first he was to enjoy three weeks' leave following what was officially described as Active Service Overseas, and went down to Biggin Hill, where he found his greatcoat still hanging on the peg where he had left it. He stayed with the Ferguson family, looked up all his old friends and was touched to learn how pleased people were to see him rise up from the dead, as it were. Their affection almost made his French experience seem worth while. His strength was returning fast and he found, to his relief, that he could once again hold his beer. Sailor, too, was on leave, pending posting, and they agreed to go up to Sutton Bridge together, collect Alan and go shooting in The Wash. Sailor's wife went with them, plus babies and dog, all in an elderly Austin 10, using petrol which he had been saving for months. They reached their destination many hours later, after two punctures and one long session under the bonnet had sorely tried the patience of everyone in the party. The shooting, happily, turned out very well.

Johnny climbed into the cockpit of a Spitfire for the first time in ten weeks on 18 November. He had a secret fear that he might have lost his touch or even his nerve and sensed that Alan was keeping an eye on him, but to his relief he found that he had no qualms about flying again. He loved flying and (once he thought it through) realised that neither he nor the aircraft had been to blame for the disastrous end to his last flight. In fact, he found he had benefitted from his layoff: now that he was no longer so tired and preoccupied by the numerous problems of leadership in the air, his handling of the Spitfire was smoother and more accurate. He enjoyed being an instructor in courses where once he had been a pupil and often thought about 'dear old Horace' [Horbaczewski] in whose company he felt, for the first time, that he might become a first class fighter pilot. Each course lasted a month and there were ten pupils to take through a demanding programme: air-to-ground and air-to-air shooting (using the target drogue), aerial combat (using camera guns), the use of rifles and revolvers, clay pigeon shooting and ballistic theories. Archie Winskill, later Captain of the Queen's Flight and knighted, was his room-mate. Having himself escaped from France in 1940, Winskill was very interested in hearing about Johnny's adventures there and they quickly became good friends.

On 22 November Johnny learned that he had been made a member of the Distinguished Service Order. In the four years of 485 Squadron's existence, John Pattison was the only other pilot so honoured while serving with it. 'Squadron Leader Checketts', the citation reads, 'has displayed courage, fortitude and skill of a high order. He has taken part in a very large number of sorties and has proved his skill in many combats, having destroyed at least eleven enemy aircraft; he has also caused the destruction of two boats. By his exceptional keenness and fine fighting spirit, Squadron Leader Checketts has proved a source of inspiration to all.' He was among a select group of New Zealand officers invited to an afternoon party at Buckingham Palace on 1 December. Alan Deere was there and so too were some other good friends: Bill Crawford-Compton, Hawkeye Wells, Colin Gray and Desmond Scott. A few days later, he received a Christmas card from another friend, Christian Martell 'and all the 341 boys. Also my heartiest congratulations for your DSO. I have just heard about it two days ago. It is a magnificent show and I am much pleased.' Christian, an outstanding flight commander in the Alsace squadron, was once described by Alan Deere as 'a gentle giant of sixteen and a half stone, but a killer in action.'

One early pupil at Sutton Bridge was an American, Lieutenant Beeson, who arrived in December with his own Lockheed Lightning which he allowed Johnny to fly. It was the first twin-engined machine he had flown and he managed to get an airlock in the fuel line to the starboard engine. He had difficulty controlling it and was obliged to make a forced landing at Mepal (near Ely in Cambridgeshire) the home of 75 Squadron, New Zealand's bomber squadron. Delighted at finding himself and the aircraft safely on the ground among a host of fellow countrymen, he celebrated his good fortune that night at a riotous party. Neither Deere nor Beeson were much impressed, however, and he was not permitted to fly the Lightning back to Sutton Bridge. Somewhat crestfallen, therefore, and monstrously hungover, he had to make his way home in a lorry.

Off duty, Johnny and Alan Deere sometimes played golf on a superb course near Sandringham: 'Alan was a very good left-hander (still is for that matter),' recalled Johnny, 'but I often thought my golf was like a good walk spoiled.' He was much better at shooting and had some exhilarating days at many places in The Wash. As at Kenley and Biggin Hill, Johnny was always eager to meet the local people — not only in pubs, though he got to know many of them — and spent happy hours exploring such lovely towns as Peterborough, King's Lynn and Spalding. For transport he had a little racing motorcycle, a KTT Velocette, which he bought in a sadly damaged condition for thirty shillings and repaired himself. A true Southland man, Johnny was untroubled by the long, bitterly cold winter of East Anglia and enjoyed himself immensely at work and play. Whenever he felt low, which was not often, he needed only to remind himself how lucky he was to be neither dead nor rotting in a prison camp and his spirits rose instantly.

The Central Gunnery School moved to Catfoss, about twenty kilometres north of Hull in the East Riding of Yorkshire, on 23

February 1944. Staff and pupils lived in Brandesburton Hall, a grand country mansion in the nearby village of the same name, and were much more comfortable off duty than in Sutton Bridge. On duty, the weather was usually so bad that it was difficult to get through course work properly and there was little pleasure in it even for a pilot as keen as Johnny. When the weather did relent, Johnny found there was an excellent area for gunnery and bombing practice just off the coast north of Hornsea.

One typical morning — foggy, wet and miserable — he was alone at dispersal, tinkering with his beloved motorcycle, when Alan Deere rang to say that No. 4 Group (Bomber Command) Headquarters had asked for a Spitfire to fly over the airfield at Leconfield, some twelve kilometres west of Catfoss, to give the anti-aircraft gunners some shooting practice. Despite the poor weather, Johnny leapt into his aircraft and raced to Leconfield, where he hurtled low over all the gun positions, attacking them with his camera guns and doing his best to prevent the gunners from getting a clear shot at him. After shooting all his film, he noticed dozens of airmen out on the tarmac, watching him. He decided to give them a show. 'The Spitfire II was a lovely aeroplane to fly and I suppose that's what prompted me to throw it around a bit. We were told not to do that sort of thing, but I felt like it and thought what the hell: the chaps on the tarmac seem interested.' So he dived on the Halifax bombers, zoomed over the hangars and ended by scattering the spectators.

Back at Catfoss, feeling very full of himself, he found Deere on the phone. The Group Commander (Air Vice-Marshal Roderick Carr) had witnessed his performance and ordered Deere to bring the pilot responsible to Leconfield immediately. 'Old Al was bloody furious,' said Johnny. 'He called me a stupid clot and hardly spoke again all the way there.' Carr, however, greeted them warmly. A New Zealander himself, he was delighted to meet two fellow countrymen. He had enjoyed the display, he said, and so had the station commander. Alan Deere's wonderful record had, of course, been widely publicised and Johnny's achievements in 1943 were also well known, so the conversation was soon bubbling along. They all had an excellent lunch together and Johnny was invited to return any time to work with the gunners. 'You were bloody lucky,' said Alan on the way home, and Johnny agreed;

a rocket from Roderick Carr would have been bad enough, but it would have been worse to get Alan into trouble.

In April 1944, after six months out of the firing line, Johnny was thrilled to receive another operational command: Commanding Officer of 1 Squadron at North Weald. The squadron was equipped with the Hawker Typhoon, a massive, heavily-armed ground-attack aircraft, quite unlike the light and agile Spitfire which was always at its best in aerial combat at high altitude. Johnny was nevertheless keen to transfer to this type and fly once again over France, helping to end the oppression of men and women who were often in his thoughts. They were ready for combat and Johnny had planned a raid south of Paris when Group Captain P. G. Jameson, 11 Group's Operations Officer, rang to cancel it. The squadron, he said, was to be re-equipped at once with the Spitfire IX. Johnny was disappointed at missing the chance to fly the Typhoon in combat. On reflection, however, he realised that he had the experience necessary to convert his Typhoon pilots quickly and efficiently to the Spitfire and that he himself would be of more immediate use in that aircraft. To help him he had as his senior flight commander an old friend from 485 Squadron, Mick Maskill.

While the pilots were mastering their Spitfires, the squadron was suddenly posted to Ayr in Scotland for gunnery training and a few days later Johnny ended his brief but hectic association with 1 Squadron when he was promoted to Wing Commander and given command of a wing of three Spitfire Vb squadrons — one British (130), one Polish (303) and one Canadian (402) — at Horne, a hastily-improvised airfield about twenty kilometres south-west of Biggin Hill. The fighter force had been re-organised in November 1943, with Fighter Command re-named Air Defence of Great Britain (ADGB) and a large number of squadrons transferred to the newly-created 2nd Tactical Air Force. As soon as the invasion of Occupied Europe began, the Horne Wing (part of ADGB) was to support the expeditionary force in the lodgement area across the Channel, as well as being on call should the Luftwaffe mount counter attacks on England.

Johnny managed to get Doug Brown, one of his old New Zealand mates, into 130 Squadron as a flight commander. 'Bruno was a wonderful bloke,' he thought, 'a most experienced fighter pilot and a jolly good leader' with a gift for managing men firmly but pleasantly. He proved a great help in maintaining the morale and efficiency of the whole wing. A nearby Canadian hospital 'adopted' Johnny's wing and so the pilots were able to bathe or shower in comfort, but nothing could be done about the food. Horne was a temporary camp, set up specifically to cover the invasion period, and its facilities, consequently, were basic. Yet even though everyone was living in tiny tents, packed tightly together, there were no complaints throughout that tense, exciting month of May, while final preparations were being made for the invasion. As wing leader, Johnny was relatively comfortable in that his tent was pitched on dry ground sheltered by a thick hedge and close to the cooking tent. Moreover, his new rank entitled him to an official car — a clapped-out Vauxhall — which, when strategically parked, provided further protection. He promptly sold his little motorcycle to a Canadian pilot for five pounds, a handsome profit. But he had few chances to enjoy car or profit, because in May he spent over sixty hours in the air, flying twenty-four fighter sweeps or escorts of medium bombers (Mitchells, Bostons and Marauders).

Although few enemy aircraft were encountered, Johnny and his pilots were often in greater danger than in 1943 because most missions were flown at low level and ground fire was even more intense and accurate. He was reminded of a wise warning which René Mouchotte used to recall from his Northolt days: 'When you are unlucky enough to be singled out by an ill-disposed gunner in the enemy ack-ack,' it read, 'and he is chasing you hard with his shells, zig-zag: but above all arrange matters so that you are always in the zag when he fires at you in the zig, or in the zig when he fires in the zag.' Several good men were lost for little obvious return — Johnny himself shot up a few airfield buildings and lorries — but the bombers did much better than in 1943: there were now plenty of them, they were more skilfully flown and far more accurate in their bombing.

Johnny was thrilled by the opportunity to lead such an international array of highly-trained, battle-worthy airmen in a cause which inspired them all, the overthrow of one of history's cruellest régimes. He never doubted the justice of that cause, for which he had travelled halfway round the world and risked his life on numerous occasions, but his personal experience of the terror and misery inflicted by the Nazis hardened him. Skirmishing over the Channel and the French coast, he realised, would never bring them down. There was, in fact, a temptation to regard that skirmishing as an end in itself — a dangerous but nevertheless exciting and even enjoyable game — while forgetting that down below decent, kindly people like those at home suffered. He therefore longed for the invasion to begin, bringing with it the chance to drive the Nazis out of France and all the other countries they had so shamelessly occupied.

On 5 June 1944, Johnny was summoned to a heavily-guarded meeting at Tangmere with other senior operational commanders, told that the invasion would begin next morning and that he must not disclose this information to his men before midnight. For the rest of that day, he had to hug this wonderful secret to himself, feeling hundreds of eyes on him: it was, of course, common knowledge that an invasion was imminent, but everyone at Horne now knew that he knew precisely when it would begin. Midnight came at last, he assembled his men and never had a more attentive audience. After his opening words, loud cheers rolled round the camp and it was some time before he could get on with the briefing. The mood, he remembered, was unrepeatable: every emotion was felt, as intensely as possible and all at the same time. Everyone was laughing, weeping, shouting and dancing about; Canadians, Poles and Britons were all slapping each other on the back and, for a moment, they were indeed a band of brothers.

Before first light on D-Day, they were over Caen, protecting a mighty fleet of bombers and gliders carrying paratroops to drop behind the beachhead. The waters off the Normandy coast were already covered with ships and landing craft and the sky was full of British and American aircraft. Although the Luftwaffe was conspicuously absent, Johnny and his men were in constant danger from fierce ship and ground fire. Seamen and soldiers, whether Allied or German, seemed to be united in regarding all aircraft as fair game and the barrage they jointly hurled into the air 'was a truly awe-inspiring sight — well worth seeing', he later wrote, 'if not worth getting in front of'. Complaints were lodged and promises made to look first and fire second, but the situation actually worsened during the afternoon. Johnny's wing was supposed to help troops fighting on the eastern beaches, but their fire — combined with that of the ships lying off shore and the German defenders — drove the Spitfires away. On that unique day, however, the amazing scenes below him were so enthralling that he felt neither fear nor resentment until later. He hunted German troops, one-man submarines and high-speed launches diligently, but without much success. By evening, he was exhausted, having flown a total of seven hours and thirty-five minutes in four separate missions and collected quite a few bullet holes from friends and enemies alike.

'Lots more bloody flak from our own ships', Johnny wrote in his log book next day. The Spitfires flew over the landing areas from dawn to dusk, suffering much damage and several casualties from ground fire which became more intense and accurate by the hour. Few German fighters were about, but Johnny did manage to close with a lone Me 109 on 8 June. He chased it far inland, hitting it repeatedly with machine-gun fire (his cannons having jammed) before shortage of fuel forced him to turn back. While flying over the Channel towards England, he was hit by fire from British ships and for several anxious minutes thought he would have to take to his parachute for the third time. Fortunately, he managed to hold his badly-damaged machine in the air long enough to reach home and put it down safely. It was during this sortie that he heard Doug Brown complaining bitterly to the fighter direction tender about fire from British and American ships. Allied aircraft, he said, were very plainly marked 'and if you can't stop our own people shooting at us, I'm bloody well going home!' Johnny thought this most amusing, until he himself was hit.

According to the official despatch of Sir Trafford Leigh-Mallory, commander of the Allied Expeditionary Air Force, the first British squadrons to land in France since 1940 were two of Johnny's: 130 and 303, which put down at noon on 10 June on a strip in the Gold landing area (around Verplage). Johnny himself landed in France — intentionally this time — on the 12th, on a hastily-improvised airstrip within the beachhead near Caen. He was almost out of fuel and taxied towards a petrol dump, threading his way between the bodies of soldiers, most of them German, until he saw some airmen in a slit trench signalling to him. He switched off and as he eased himself out of the cockpit heard one of the men call out: 'Get down, you fool. There's a Hun sniper in the trees over there.' Thus advised, he rapidly abandoned his Spitfire and dived smartly into the trench. The sniper, he was told, had picked off several men that morning, but a few minutes later Johnny saw him shot out of the trees by some soldiers. He managed to souvenir the sniper's rifle and flourished it confidently while the airmen filled his petrol tank. All told, he spent over six hours in the air that day and was so tired by the end that he was flying like an automaton.

Leading his squadrons at tree-top height behind the German lines, Johnny and his men found many targets during the next few days — lorries, buses, cars and troop columns — but none were easy to hit and ground fire took its toll of aircraft and pilots' nerves. Nevertheless, they were thankful for two mercies: the Luftwaffe offered no serious interference and Allied gunners shot at them less frequently. On 15 June he was asked by a reporter for his impressions of Normandy. 'During the day,' he said, 'it is almost like flying over the quiet English countryside. Sometimes you can see a belch of flame coming from one clump of trees and an answering flash from another clump and you know that a tank battle is progressing. At night you can see gun flashes stabbing the darkness. Here and there, of course, there are towns afire. Caen, for instance, is just a mass of flames and St Lo is a heap of rubble. It is as flat as a bun.' That afternoon, he told the reporter, he had led one of his squadrons on patrol over Carentan. 'There was no sign of enemy aircraft and so we looked for transport. I saw some lorries pulled into a roadside under poplar trees and led down a section of Poles. We shot them up and left them afire.'

Next day, however, a new enemy caught them completely unawares in England: the V1 flying bomb or 'Doodle Bug'. Johnny had just emerged from his tent at about 6 a.m. when he heard its strange noise for the first time: described by a member of the Royal Observer Corps as 'like a Model T Ford going up a hill'. It seemed to be heading straight for him, so he threw himself into the ditch behind his tent. The bomb roared overhead, its engine cut and there was a short, dreadful silence before it exploded in the hills south of Caterham. Though they were very fast — for a Spitfire Vb — he managed to destroy two in the next three days. Deciding that one of their flight paths might lie over Horne, he had two machine-guns set up in front of his Intelligence Officer's hut and stuck close to these guns whenever he was not flying, but no Doodle Bugs appeared. Then, while he was paying a brief visit to Kenley to see about replacement aircraft, one did fly over the airfield and the Intelligence Officer shot it down, neatly and efficiently. 'I didn't know whether to laugh or cry,' he wrote later.

Johnny's wing moved from Horne on 19 June to Westhampnett, a satellite airfield of Tangmere in Sussex. At that time, there was fierce fighting around Caen — the hinge upon which the Allied armies hoped to turn eastward towards Paris and Germany — and his Spitfires were busy every day attacking troops and transport moving into the battle area. All their flying was done at tree-top level, well inside machine-gun range, but at least the Luftwaffe did not trouble them. It was dangerous work, more dangerous than dogfighting high in the sky even against odds, but it was also valuable work: destroying lorries and cars or forcing them off the road; compelling troops to scurry for cover in hedges or ditches and keeping them there, away from the front. Johnny flew twenty-eight missions in twenty-three days after D-Day, amounting to more than seventy-seven hours in the air, almost all of them in close-support work over the beachheads. 'Hun flak very accurate' he noted in his log book on the 28th. 'I was very frightened. Hit and destroyed two trucks.'

Early in July, however, his wing enjoyed a welcome change: escorting heavy bombers and sweeping for enemy fighters as far inland as Chartres, 150 kilometres from the sea. On the 7th Johnny helped to escort 460 Lancasters and Halifaxes in an attack on Caen. It was the first time he had seen a full-size British heavy bomber raid, complete with an elaborate display of multi-coloured marker flares, and he was suitably impressed. The bombing was almost painfully accurate, in the absence of fighter opposition, and he wondered how anyone in Caen — French or German — could survive. Bad weather then grounded the wing for nearly a week of blessed rest until 13 July when it accompanied 180 Lancasters sent to bomb marshalling yards in Paris. Johnny, who had often escorted American bombers in 1943 and greatly admired their compact formations, was pleased to see that even though British bombers scattered all over the sky (because they were untrained in daylight formation flying) they nevertheless flew bravely over the target despite heavy flak and bombed accurately. His wing again escorted a heavy raid on Caen, this time by 1,000 British bombers, on the 18th. In the absence of Luftwaffe opposition he had nothing to do but watch, fascinated and appalled, and wonder what there could be left to destroy in that town. Short of fuel, he landed near Caen once the bombers had departed and watched a follow-up raid by Marauders. He was even more appalled, now that he could hear the noise of ceaseless anti-aircraft fire and feel the earth shake as dozens of bombs exploded; worse still, he could see numerous dead bodies (soldiers and civilians) scattered among wrecked buildings, vehicles and weapons.

During July Johnny flew nearly forty-eight hours, mostly on escort duties or ground strafing. Only once, on the 26th, did he see a substantial number of German fighters: 'While escorting eighteen Mitchells to Alençon at 15,000 feet, we ran into twenty Me 109s,' he recalled. 'It was dreadful. Our Spitfire Vbs were useless at that height and I was most disappointed at not being able to tackle them: they simply ran away from us.' On the way home, he landed at Crepon, Bazenville (a temporary airstrip) and found Johnnie Johnson, now at the height of his fame as a fighter pilot, in charge. Johnson listened sympathetically to his sad story and gave him a beer mug as a consolation prize. Thus inspired, Johnny had his first aerial victory as a wing leader on 1 August, while returning from an escort to Livarot, shooting down an Me 109. Otherwise, he carried on with the established routine and spent sixty-six hours in the air during that month, escorting bomber formations of all shapes and sizes to numerous targets within Spitfire range and shooting up 'targets of opportunity' on the ground.

Although the Luftwaffe seemed finished, this was certainly not true of the German army. Anti-aircraft and small arms fire remained as intense and accurate as ever. There were few days during that summer when he did not fly over France or the Low Countries at least once and on practically every mission he saw bombers trailing smoke or flames. Sometimes they were able to head for home and he could escort them, willing the pilots to hold their altitude and keep control; sometimes there was nothing he could do except watch as a stricken bomber spiralled gently down until it was lost to sight; at other times a bomber would suddenly explode, apparently silently, into a gigantic black cloud spattered with brilliant colours. And yet anti-aircraft fire did not frighten him. Flying fast and high in a tiny Spitfire, it really would be bad luck — but quite painless, he thought — to suffer a direct hit. Ground strafing, however, was a different matter and he schooled himself not to think about it. 'If once you started reckoning up,' he said, 'how many bullets and shells those well-trained Hun gunners were aiming at you personally from a very handy range — well, you just wouldn't go through with it.' But he did go through with it, day after day, knowing that it was necessary work: the lorries, motorcycles, barges and troops shot up were all bonuses, incidental to the main purpose of closing to the German Army as many roads as possible for as long as possible throughout the daylight hours.

On 28 August the wing moved again, from Westhampnett to Merston, another satellite of Tangmere, where it was better placed to escort bombers attacking flying-bomb launching and storage sites in the Pas de Calais. As usual, he was most impressed by the accuracy with which Lancasters and Halifaxes were able to mark and hit targets more than seven kilometres below them, even allowing that daylight and the absence of enemy fighters were wonderful aids to concentration. At the end of August, to his great sorrow, Flight Lieutenant Stasik of 303 (Polish) Squadron was killed by ground fire near Ostend. Having flown more often with that squadron than with his other units (because it was so short of pilots), he had got to know his Polish pilots well. They were grand fellows, he wrote, generous and kind, courteous to others, and the most terrific fighter pilots. Their sense of discipline, on the ground and in the air, was very strict. Their morale was high and (off duty) their choral singing was simply marvellous. He was — and is — very proud to have had such brave and skilful airmen under his command. Stasik, he thought, would have compared favourably with the best even in that famous squadron. He was a courteous, cheerful man and, despite language problems, they had become good friends.

Johnny also enjoyed flying with 130 Squadron, particularly when he had Bruno (Doug Brown) with him: he was reminded of good days at Kenley and Biggin Hill, made all the sweeter by the absence of the Luftwaffe. By September, as the Allied armies moved east and north-east out of Normandy, so Johnny's wing was more regularly employed on missions at maximum range, escorting massive bomber attacks on targets in western Germany. There the flak was so intense that it seemed no longer very unlikely that his Spitfire might be hit, but — sticking to his principles — he refused to think about what the Germans might do to him and concentrated instead on what he was determined to do to them.

CHAPTER ELEVEN

# Learning Again:
# September 1944
# to November 1945

Operation Market Garden was launched on 17 September 1944. Three airborne divisions were dropped, during three days, with orders to seize seven bridges over rivers and canals on the road between Eindhoven and Arnhem, a distance of some seventy-two kilometres. They were to hold these positions until units of the British 2nd Army came up from the Belgian frontier. That army would then be able to lead an allied drive north through Holland to Arnhem, outflank the Siegfried Line (the German frontier defences) and strike east into the Ruhr and across the north German plain, ending the European war, if all went well, by Christmas. The vital bridge over the Lower Rhine at Arnhem, however, proved 'a bridge too far', as Lieutenant-General Sir Frederick Browning, commander of the British 1st Airborne Corps, had foreseen. British and Polish paratroops, landed about twelve kilometres from that massive road bridge, and found strong German forces around them. British ground forces and two American paratroop divisions, landed farther south, were prevented from linking up with their beleaguered allies at Arnhem, although they did capture several bridges. The operation nevertheless failed in its primary objective and with its failure ended all hopes of finishing the European war in 1944.

Johnny and his wing flew cover for transports and gliders carrying paratroops taking part in the operation on 18 September. Later that day, they escorted 400 Liberators carrying supplies to those troops. Low cloud and fog helped keep the Luftwaffe away, but did nothing to silence anti-aircraft fire, which was as dangerous as ever. Many transports and gliders were brought down and Johnny saw several gliders drifting near the Dutch coast with soldiers clinging to them. He did all he could to help by taking his Spitfires down to attack flak posts, armed barges and motor transport. It soon became clear, however, that the Allied troops were facing defeat. On 25 September he led his wing into a fierce action over Arnhem with about fifty German fighters. The wing suffered no losses and claimed four victories, in one of which he shared. As he described it at the time: 'The Hun popped out from cloud and came down to attack one of my pilots. We nipped in smartly and I had first go at him. He jettisoned his hood and something fell off. Then one of the flight commanders, an Englishman, followed the enemy down and completed the kill.'

Next day, Johnny noted in his log book: 'My last sweep. Have been taken off operations.' He was certainly due for a rest. During the last 148 days he had flown 115 missions, spending 301 hours in the air. Johnny thus ended his operational career with fourteen confirmed victories to his credit (plus one shared) as well as claiming three probable victories and at least eleven enemy aircraft damaged; he also destroyed two flying bombs, shot up several E-boats and flak barges and attacked numerous ground targets — airfield buildings, railway and port installations, factories, military transports and troop concentrations. Far away in Invercargill, the last operational flight of 'one of New Zealand's most distinguished pilots' was reported in the *Southland Times* on 28 September. It was about this time that the Air Ministry selected him as one of New Zealand's six leading fighter aces and commissioned an eminent artist, William Dring, to paint his portrait. Johnny, no doubt embarrassed at being singled out for this unusual honour, protested that he was too busy to sit and tried to send Dring away. But a terse Air Ministry signal swiftly quelled him. He is glad now that it did, for the portrait (given to Natalie 'on permanent loan' by Air Vice-Marshal M. F. Calder while Chief of Air Staff, Royal New Zealand Air Force) is a good one. A year later, when the war was over, Sailor Malan would single out Johnny and Bill Crawford-Compton as New Zealanders 'who both fought brilliantly in Normandy'. Such praise from one of the war's great fighter pilots and commanders was worth savouring.

Ever since escaping from France and particularly since his return to active service, Johnny had longed for the day when he could say a proper thank you to all those brave, generous men and women who saved him from prison or execution and made it possible for him to stay in the fight. Amiens and Abbeville having been liberated on 12 September 1944, he flew to an airfield nearby and Alan Deere (who was based there) agreed to drive him to Tours-en-Vimeu, where Marcel and Charlotte Lecointe had risked their lives for his sake exactly twelve months earlier. On arriving in the village, Johnny was distressed to learn that they had been arrested by the Gestapo in December 1943 and sent to concentration camps, Marcel to Buchenwald, Charlotte to Mauthausen. No-one knew whether they were alive or dead. He heard this shocking news from the boy who took him on his bicycle to the wood where he first hid; it was confirmed by the village priest, his fellow-guest at Marcel's twenty-sixth birthday party. The priest produced a bottle of champagne, the New Zealanders were treated to an excellent dinner by the villagers, but what should have been a memorable occasion was ruined for Johnny by the absence of his good friends. At about 2 a.m. next morning, Alan drove him back to his airfield and at first light he flew sadly home to Westhampnett.

Almost a year passed before Johnny was able to learn more. While visiting Bill Kemp, Commanding Officer of 487 (New Zealand) Squadron at Cambrai in August 1945, he borrowed a jeep and drove to Tours-en-Vimeu, where he found to his great joy that Marcel and Charlotte were back in their own home. They had not long been free and both were gaunt and listless, though obviously glad to see him and trying to be cheerful. Johnny took them to a farmhouse near Amiens, where they all enjoyed a reunion of men and women liberated from concentration camps. The rejoicing, muted as it was, served only to distress Johnny, thinking of the Nazi victims for whom the war lasted too long. The determination of Marcel, Charlotte and their friends to regard Johnny as something special served only to distress him further. 'They were the special ones,' he says, 'not me.' After a bitter-sweet evening, he took the Lecointes home. They parted sadly, with much still to say on either side. Johnny returned to Cambrai and then to New Zealand and though a few letters were exchanged during the next year or two, he never saw them again.

Calais fell on 1 October while he was visiting a fellow New Zealander, Group Captain Desmond Scott, commander of a wing of four Typhoon squadrons at Merville, near Lille. They drove into the wrecked city and came upon a German underground bunker, Scott recalled, 'full of frozen pork, blocks of apple sauce, frozen green peas and case upon case of Portuguese sardines. Small mobs of young pigs were running loose amongst the bomb-shattered buildings. We caught one of these little porkers, put him in a box, and filled the rest of the station wagon with cases of sardines.' They returned to Merville with their loot and that night he and Johnny went to Lille, met Alan Deere (now a staff officer in 84 Group), visited a night club and 'drank more than was good for us'. Next day, wrote Scott, while they were flying in an Auster over Lille, Johnny 'hung his head out of the window into the slipstream and appeared to be asleep. I could not resist the temptation to pull my 38 calibre Smith and Wesson from its holster, put my arm out past his head, and pull the trigger. He shot bolt upright, his bloodshot eyes like pink saucers. Johnny was six years my senior, but being very much a boy at heart we were soon rocking the little plane with our laughter.'

Three weeks later, Johnny learned that he had been awarded the Silver Star, the third highest decoration for gallantry offered by the United States Armed Forces. 'During the sixty missions in which he has flown fighter escort for USAAF bombers,' reads the citation, 'only two bombers have been lost in spite of heavy fighter opposition. The courage, aggressiveness and skill displayed by Acting Wing Commander Checketts reflect the highest credit upon himself and the Armed Forces of his country.' Johnny was also honoured by his old Polish colleagues. Members of 303 Squadron, he was told by the Chief Polish Liaison Officer at Fighter Command Headquarters, 'valued your leadership and deeply regretted the separation which inevitably occurs.' He took part in twenty-five of that squadron's operational sorties, efforts that were recognised by the award of the Cross of Valour and the Polish flying badge, with green wreath. 'It is a fine record and we are proud to count you amongst the aces of the Polish Air Force', wrote its Commander-in-Chief, Air Vice-Marshal Izycki, after the war.

Johnny's reward for five months of intensive operations was a plum posting in October to the Central Fighter Establishment at Wittering, about sixteen kilometres west of Peterborough. There he found himself part of a small group charged to analyse fighter tactics: Wing Commander Erik Haabjoern, a Norwegian Typhoon pilot, was to concentrate on low-level co-operation with ground forces; Wing Commander Robin Johnston and an American officer, Lieutenant-Colonel Randy Keator (both Mustang pilots) were to specialise in the duties of long-range escort fighters; and Johnny was to study the role of short-range high-altitude fighters.

They were all sent to Italy early in November. Johnny was to fly out in a Spitfire fitted with a new type of internal fuel tank while the rest followed in a de Havilland Dominie. When they reached Paris, however, Keator awarded himself a quick circuit in the Spitfire and contrived to land it on its nose. Johnny was therefore obliged to join his fellow experts in the Dominie. From Paris, they flew to Dijon where they had an unforgettable night at the opera. The house was bitterly cold and the singers so thoroughly wrapped up (in street clothes) that they could scarcely move let alone sing properly, and yet the audience sat entranced because at long last the Germans had gone and, for the time being, that in itself was enough to ensure a festival atmosphere and a warm welcome for four Allied pilots.

From Dijon, they flew via Lyons, Marseille, Borgo (in Corsica), Naples and Rome to Rimini, headquarters of the Desert Air Force, where they were splendidly entertained to dinner — in a tent — by the AOC, Air Vice-Marshal William Dickson, 'a very charming bloke', who wanted to hear all about life in England and their part in the Normandy invasion. The New Zealand Division was resting about 480 kilometres farther south, midway between Bari and Taranto, after prolonged, severe fighting, and Johnny managed to track down his brother Alan (a gunner in that division) whom he had not seen for four years. The Commanding Officer of Alan's unit was Major Charlie Baker of Dunedin, whose brother Reg had saved Johnny's life when he was shot down into the Channel in May 1942. Charlie readily granted Alan forty-eight hours' leave and Johnny reckons they were the wildest forty-eight hours of his life. Before that happy reunion, Johnny had taken a Spitfire of the Desert Air Force down to Fano (south of Rimini) and persuaded Wing Commander Hugh (Cocky) Dundas, a famous Battle of Britain pilot who commanded a wing there, to let him take part in an armed reconnaissance. He was thrilled to be on active service again, however briefly, but no enemies were found in the air or on the ground. Leaving Rimini on 18 November, he spent twelve days flying home to Wittering. Apart from seeing Alan again, he had not enjoyed his visit to Italy: snow or mud everywhere, freezing temperatures and all the ruin and misery caused by long, hard fighting.

Johnny spent December at Wittering, doing little flying but plenty of talking and writing about fighter tactics. Although he already missed operational duties very much, there was at least more time for fun. On one occasion, he went with Hawkeye Wells (his old squadron commander, now also stationed at Wittering) to Milfield in Northumberland where they enjoyed some shooting. On another, his old Kenley station commander, Batchy Atcherley, having organised 'a fearful thrash' on Christmas Day, made all his officers play rugby in the snow next morning. Even though Johnny felt as frail as his comrades, he had to show enthusiasm and ability to uphold the honour of New Zealand; he managed it, but only just, and rarely played rugby again.

During January 1945 the Central Fighter Establishment moved from Wittering to Tangmere. As High Level Tactics Officer in the Tactics Branch, he was able to fly a wide variety of aircraft, Allied and German, in the line of duty as well as pleasure. Apart from Spitfires, Mosquitos, Martinets, Proctors, Ansons and Stinsons, he flew several German types — the Messerschmitt 110 (so heavy and slow that it almost made him feel sorry for those airmen who had flown it in daylight against the best British and American fighters), the Junkers 88 (a much superior aircraft, very responsive, remarkably quick for its size and power) and, best of all, a Messerschmitt 109G-14. 'It was very good,' he remembered. 'I was asked to attack some Grumman Hellcat fighters with it and enjoyed myself immensely: they were so slow and clumsy by comparison that I could have shot them all down quite easily.' The Luftwaffe had launched a well-planned attack on Allied airfields in Belgium and Holland on New Year's Day that achieved complete surprise. As an official fighter tactics expert, Johnny therefore had an excellent reason for spending a week in February in Brussels, asking pilots and staff officers to explain what had happened from both the Allied and German points of view. On 27 February he had the great thrill of flying a jet aircraft for the first time: a Gloster Meteor. He managed to fly unofficially with his old wing on one or two fighter sweeps and escorts, having been warned that he would be in serious trouble if he got shot down and killed.

While at Tangmere, Johnny met several German airmen who had been sent there for interrogation. Among them was Oberstleutnant Arnold Bauer, whose record as a fighter pilot went back ten years, to the Spanish Civil War: during that time, he told Johnny, he had been shot down thirty-two times. He also told him that if it had not been for a desperate shortage of aviation fuel since the middle of 1944, which severely restricted the training of new pilots as well as the operational flying of experienced pilots, the Luftwaffe would have put up a much better defence after D-Day. Johnny made no answer, but privately he thought the Germans had done well enough as it was. He liked Bauer: 'You could have put him in a Royal Air Force uniform and he'd have been one of us. He had a pleasant manner and a real fighter pilot outlook.' But he did not like Hans-Ulrich Rudel, the famous Stuka pilot who destroyed an amazing number of Russian tanks: 'I admit that he must have had plenty of courage and skill — plenty of luck as well — but he was a true Nazi, arrogant and full of hate; he could never have worn our uniform. I detested him.'

In January 1945, meanwhile, Johnny suffered a harrowing experience when at last he managed to return to Brittany. He had already learned from her parents that his dear friend, Agnès de Nanteuil, was dead and could now only commiserate and hear at first hand what had become of her. In March 1944, he was told, after nearly four years of active resistance, Agnès was betrayed in Vannes, her home town. The Gestapo interrogated her with their customary brutality twelve times during the next five months in vain attempts to discover the names of those with whom she had worked. On 6 August she attempted to escape while an air raid distracted the prison guards, but they shot and wounded her. Dumped in a cattle truck with other known resisters and denied vital medical attention, she died a week later in the railway station at Paray-le-Monial, some sixty-four kilometres north-east of Vichy. She was just twenty-one. 'She was wounded in my arms,' wrote Catherine, her sister, to Johnny in August 1945, 'and as long as I live I remember this wonderful courage in front of death and her everlasting smile which help me so much during difficult moments of the life.'

Although the European war was clearly in its last stages, the war against Japan seemed likely to last another year or more. Since he was no longer needed in the front line against Germany, Johnny thought he would be more use fighting with the Royal New Zealand Air Force against the Japanese in the Pacific Islands than stooging about in every aircraft that came his way in England. He therefore asked for a transfer, but Hugh Saunders refused to let him go. Instead, he sent him in April to Watchfield near Swindon to undertake a short instrument flying course as a preliminary to posting him to the Empire Central Flying School at Hullavington in Wiltshire, about thirty kilometres north-east of Bristol. There, in the words of the school's prospectus, he would 'study the art of flying and examine the methods of teaching that art'. It was not a school for training instructors. On the contrary, it was open only to those who were already experienced operational pilots and therefore able to benefit from the gospel of 'limit flying': that is, to seek mastery of an aircraft by taking — not avoiding — risks, by learning precisely how far to go at any speed, altitude or attitude. The school 'has been described both as a university of flying and as a parliament of flying . . . It resembles a university in that it sets out to provide learning of a high order for those who seek it [and] a parliament in that much of its work is done by discussion. . . .'

Johnny was interviewed on arriving at Hullavington by the Chief Ground Instructor, an elderly wing commander with a supercilious manner: 'Oh dear,' he drawled, looking at Johnny's record, 'a fighter pilot. They never do any good here. Simply not up to it, I'm afraid.' At this time, Johnny was in a cantankerous mood, quite prepared to do badly at Hullavington, make a pest of himself and get sent home to New Zealand that way. But these dismissive words brought out a perverse streak in his nature and he decided to show everyone what a mere fighter pilot could do. He knew perfectly well that from a civilian or peacetime point of view, his airmanship was effective rather than elegant. It could hardly be otherwise after years of dogfighting and ground strafing, but he had always loved flying as a pure skill and relished the opportunity now given him to show that he was no rough-and-ready hack. With neither enemy fighters nor anti-aircraft fire to worry about, no restrictions on the use of radio aids and no obligation to fly at low level in bad weather, it should be easy, he thought. And it was: between April and August, he flew numerous different types of aircraft, from single-engined fighters to four-engined bombers (not forgetting the odd Gladiator biplane, Hotspur glider and even a sailplane) and handled every one as gently as a new-born babe. At the end of the course, to no-one's surprise except his own, he was awarded a Distinguished Pass.

The Navigation Officer at Hullavington was the famous New Zealand airman and seaman, Francis Chichester. He devised methods to teach 'nought feet navigation' for pilots flying over enemy territory when they might be unable to take their eyes off the ground ahead and had to jink constantly to avoid anti-aircraft fire. 'It amounted to map reading without maps,' Chichester wrote, 'in other words all the map reading had to be done on the ground before taking off. It sounds an impossible requirement but, with the right methods, and plenty of drill, pilots could find a haystack fifty miles off while dodging about all the way to it.' He and Johnny became lifelong friends. They would cycle to the Doone river, near the beautiful village of Castle Combe, to fish and talk together by the hour. 'Francis taught me more about navigation than I ever thought I could learn — and until I met him, I reckoned I was a good navigator.' In February 1947, Chichester would write: 'New Zealand does not seem to have made nearly as much fuss of Johnny Checketts as I expected. I regard him as one of the most interesting and forceful New Zealand personalities I have met. His flying was top-line stuff and his escape from France when shot down held the Empire Central Flying School completely enthralled while he recounted it.'

The Chief Flying Instructor was a South African, Lieutenant Colonel Jim Kelly. One day, he asked Johnny for his opinion of the Spitfire IX. Johnny gave it at great length, with plenty of enthusiasm and nostalgia, and was summoned next day to Kelly's office. Douglas Bader (whom Johnny had already encountered at Tangmere, finding him brusque and opinionated) was there, and Johnny was invited to brief the great man on the handling and performance characteristics of the Mark IX as compared with the Mark V, which Bader had been flying when he was shot down in August 1941. 'He actually listened to what I had to say — which made a nice change — and then took off. Even though he'd been grounded for nearly four years, he was obviously a very fine pilot and we seemed to get on well after that.'

The war against Japan ended in August and the Royal New Zealand Air Force authorities ordered Johnny to go to Brighton as soon as he completed his course at Hullavington and prepare for repatriation. He would retain the rank — but not the pay — of a wing commander. 'I thought this a wee bit on the nose,' he recalls, 'however, that's the hierarchy for you.' Before reporting to Brighton, he managed to wangle himself a month at Andrews Field, a former United States Army Air Force base in Essex, where he enjoyed a splendid reunion with 303 (Polish) Squadron and the station commander, none other than his good friend Alan Deere. That squadron was then equipped with the Mustang and Johnny was thrilled to have a chance to fly that magnificent fighter again in the company of dear friends with no distraction from either the Luftwaffe or flak batteries. He was also able to enjoy their company in the Mess each evening with no worries about getting the chop next morning. He spent three happy days in London with the Ferguson family, with Alan and his fiancée, Joan Fenton (they were to marry on 18 September), with Bobby Page and some of his old pilots in the Kimul Club and then, on 4 September, it was time to catch a train to Prestwick near Ayr in Scotland and begin the long journey home.

From Prestwick, Johnny flew as a passenger in a Liberator to Montreal in Canada. He was in the air for over sixteen hours. By far the longest, coldest, most uncomfortable flight of his life, it made him thank his lucky stars that he had not spent the war in Bomber or Coastal Command. The aircraft landed at 5.30 a.m. and Johnny gladly left the Liberator there. It was pitch black still, but he managed to stagger round the side of a hangar, carrying his case and shotgun. To his astonishment, he suddenly came upon a blaze of lights: runways and buildings were all clearly visible and instinctively he looked up, listening for the drone of German bombers. For the last four years, the only lights he had seen at night had come from burning buildings and so he stood gazing at these lights, as helplessly fascinated as a rabbit. He found a café on the airfield and there received a second shock. It was full of food and drink of all kinds: bacon, tomatoes, eggs, sausages, fish, milk, orange juice and real coffee displayed in abundance, producing delicious aromas which he had forgotten existed. Once again, he found himself staring, helplessly fascinated. Sadly, his stomach had been trained for years to accept only basic necessities and was quite unable to cope with a feast of tasty food. Having done what he could, however, he telephoned Group Captain Trevor (Tiny) White, Chief Liaison Officer at the New Zealand Air Mission in Ottawa and flew there later that day. He spent ten days with Tiny and his wife in that city. His record as an outstanding fighter pilot — one who had, moreover, had a Canadian squadron under his command — ensured that he was generously wined and dined wherever he went. Thus inspired, it did not take him long to learn how to handle good food once again.

On 17 September Johnny flew back to Montreal and thence to Washington D.C. for a couple of days before crossing the continent by easy stages in a Dakota to San Diego, California, where he had his second uncomfortable brush with American military policemen. He was travelling in uniform and someone stole his hat; when he went sightseeing without it he was promptly ordered off the streets even though he was not an American serviceman and the war was over. He flew from San Diego to Hawaii in another Liberator, a flight of some thirteen hours. For one whole day, he lazed on the beach under a hot sun, trying to remember when he had last enjoyed that simple pleasure. Then it was time to climb aboard the Liberator again for three more long flights: eight hours to Canton Island, another eight to Fiji and then a final eight to Whenuapai. He arrived in New Zealand on 1 October 1945, more than four years after his excited but apprehensive departure to take part in a war that seemed likely to end in a Fascist victory. He had officially served overseas for 1,532 days, earning a gratuity of £191 10s (2s 6d per day): a goodly sum for those days.

To his delight, Johnny found his father waiting for him in the reception lounge; to his surprise, some reporters were also there who asked him at great length about his experiences and intentions. Like many New Zealanders, Johnny is extremely reticent in public and has always regarded press interviews as a chore to endure rather than a pleasure to enjoy. The *Auckland Star*, for example, found that he had a 'masterly capacity for reticence and understatement' and would only speak freely about other pilots, especially the Poles, who 'were magnificent fighters, but fought as if for a lost cause. Always ready to sacrifice their own lives, they sometimes let their tenacity get the better of their judgment.' 'Nothing could coax him into telling the story of his mysterious escape from France', complained the *Observer*; as for his future plans, he would say only that he did not intend to return to his old job as a motor mechanic.

Johnny and his father escaped at last and next day flew together in a Dominie to New Plymouth, where he was able to telephone Natalie, and then on to Wellington. There he met the Chief of Air Staff (Air Vice-Marshal Leonard Isitt) who greeted him warmly and asked him what he intended to do. Johnny replied that he would like to remain in the service. Isitt seemed pleased, but warned him that the peacetime air force would be very small and advised him to consider a transfer to the Royal Air Force: 'I said that although I loved the RAF, I loved New Zealand much more and wanted to make my career here.' He was then told that the Minister in charge of the Air Department (Freddie Jones) wished to meet him, so he trudged across to Parliament Buildings. Four hours later, having looked everywhere for Jones, he decided to wait no longer and went to the airport where he scrounged a flight in a Harvard to Blenheim and thence to Wigram and so, at long last, to Natalie's home. They had a happy reunion that evening (marred only by another press interview), but when he reported to Wigram next morning, he was told that he would be discharged immediately. The flight lieutenant in charge was brusque, Johnny was brusquer — 'I suppose I was a wee bit curt with him' — and they parted coldly, with nothing agreed or signed. Refusing to allow this bitter episode to upset him, he had a glorious week with Natalie and a whole host of friends and relatives, both actual and potential.

The Checketts then travelled by train to Invercargill and Johnny was able to sample again the horrors of such journeys in New Zealand: proceeding at little more than walking pace with numerous lengthy halts for passengers to scramble for stewed tea and stale sandwiches. The scenery, however, seemed more magnificent than ever. Heavy rain was driving across the station as they pulled into Invercargill and he was astonished to find numerous people waiting to greet him, led by the mayors of Invercargill and Dunedin. Both made speeches, expressing their pleasure at the safe return home of 'this famous man'; the crowd cheered heartily and he was obliged to respond. Next day, he was swept away to a morning tea organised by representatives of patriotic organisations, the local branch of the Returned Services Association and the Army Department. 'We are very proud of you,' said one speaker, 'you have earned a great name for Invercargill and for Southland.' Another recalled that 'Johnny was always a dare-devil and dare-devils seem to do pretty well when they go into the air.' A third reminded the audience, amid laughter and cheers, that he had been a particularly lively member of the 'wild motor-cycle platoon' of the Southland Regiment before the war. At this and other functions during the next few days, he replied as well as he could, praising the deeds of all the Allied airmen with whom he had served and remaining mute about his own. He was quite overcome, not realising the strength of the reputation he had earned, and was still trying to come to terms with it when an urgent signal arrived from Wellington ordering him to report there immediately.

Puzzled and annoyed in equal measure, Johnny was flown to the capital in a Harvard sent especially from Wigram. He was swept into the presence of Freddie Jones, who held out his hand and said: 'Welcome home, I always welcome my heroes home and I expected you to come in sooner. I'll get your member and he can show you round the House.' Johnny replied politely, and with these civilities out of the way, waited for the minister to disclose the real reason for dragging him at considerable inconvenience and expense back to Wellington. Presently he realised that there was no reason; Jones had said all he wanted to say. Taking a deep breath and forcing himself to speak slowly and calmly, he said that he had not seen his family and friends for over four years and regretted that he had been called away from them after only a couple of days for such a trivial reason. Quite unabashed, Jones smiled and said: 'Aw, don't worry about that, I always welcome my heroes home; everybody knows that.'

At that moment, fortunately, the member for Invercargill (Bill Denham) arrived. Johnny knew him slightly: 'He used to be our milkman when I was a young fellow. He wasn't a bad sort of chap and in spite of his politics [he was a Labour politician] my father got on quite well with him.' Bill Denham took him into the so-called debating chamber where he observed the customary wrangling for some minutes: 'It was my first visit to that place and the behaviour of our rulers amazed me. I had no idea they went on like that; it was disgraceful.' Denham then took him to meet the Minister of Finance (Walter Nash) who asked him about his plans. Johnny said that he hoped to stay in the air force. 'Well, if you do,' replied Nash, 'you'll have to drop a lot of that rank. Some of you fellows got quick promotion overseas and we can't afford to pay you at that rate.' Stung by these words, his self control gave way. 'You were willing enough to pay us to die,' he snapped, 'but you're not willing to pay us to live. If ever I had a temptation to vote Labour, you've very successfully squashed it!' He stomped out of Nash's office, followed by the unfortunate Denham, who also heard the rough edge of Johnny's tongue.

Then, on 10 November 1945, came a rather more satisfying experience. He and Natalie Grover were married that day in St Matthew's Anglican Church, St Albans, Christchurch. Natalie had been a popular teacher and her pupils' parents insisted that she use their sugar and dried fruit coupons (for these items were then strictly rationed) to make a real peacetime wedding cake. Johnny, as one of the most famous and highly-decorated of New Zealand's airmen in Europe, was then a centre of attraction wherever he went. Even so, the wedding proved to be a far greater occasion than either of them expected. Very large crowds lined the approaches to St Matthew's and the ceremony was delayed for some time while the minister and his attendants arranged for as many people as possible to pack into the church.

The Guest of Honour was New Zealand's most distinguished High Commissioner in London, Mr W. J. Jordan, a man greatly admired for his devoted services throughout the war. Bill Jordan was then in New Zealand for the first time in seven years and flew specially to Christchurch for the ceremony. Several 485 Squadron pilots were present, among them Leslie White, Marty Hume, Mick Shand and James Hayter, and a telegram arrived from the Polish officers and men of 303 Squadron. A unique ornament worn by Natalie was a gold miniature Cross of Lorraine presented to Johnny by members of 341 (Alsace) Squadron at Biggin Hill and suitably inscribed to commemorate his escape from Occupied France in October 1943. Marie de Nanteuil (sister of Agnès and Catherine) wrote from Vannes in February 1946 to congratulate the Checketts on their marriage. 'I hope you will have a great and beautiful family,' she wrote, 'and your children will seem to [that is, take after] *their father*! I would like to tell only some words to your wife: Dear Madame. You have a delightful husband who has many many qualities we have appreciated when he was here. Always happy and cheerful. Your choice is perfect. My dear Johnny, all that is true, is not?'

He and Natalie were to spend their first night together at an hotel in Diamond Harbour and drove there at about 11 p.m. after a splendid reception. When they reached the hotel, however, they learned that the Government Tourist Bureau had failed to book them in. The landlord, luckily, had a vacant room and so the happy couple were spared the embarrassment of trailing round the Christchurch hotels looking for a bed on their wedding night. The landlord shouted Johnny a final drink (to go with those he had had already) and as it went down, he saw an enormous rat coming-through the door. No sooner had he foresworn alcohol for ever than he was told that it was actually a pet opossum. Although it was very friendly, Johnny has never since felt quite at ease with those animals.

Natalie discreetly withdrew, leaving him to don his pure silk pyjamas, bought for this occasion in San Diego. He then discovered that Natalie's Aunt Ina had neatly sown the front to the rear with a small Union Jack. His first instinct was to go to bed without them, but he lacked the nerve. And so, when Natalie emerged from the bathroom, she found her new husband sitting cross-legged on the bed, carefully cutting stitches with a razor blade.

## CHAPTER TWELVE

# Serving with the RNZAF: November 1945 to March 1955

Johnny and Natalie enjoyed two happy days at Diamond Harbour before flying to Auckland from Harewood in an RNZAF Dakota, spending their first evening in that city with Doug Brown and his family. Johnny was delighted to introduce Natalie to such a good friend and Natalie, for her part, was eager to meet a man with whom her husband had shared experiences which already seemed incredible. Then and later, she found it easy to believe their numerous vivid reminiscences (suitably censored for her ears), but it was much more difficult to believe that these men, apparently so light-hearted and carefree, had once been such accomplished killers.

There was a severe shortage of housing in New Zealand at that time and so, on returning to Christchurch, the Checketts lived with Natalie's parents until they found suitable service quarters for themselves. Johnny was appointed Administrative Officer at Wigram and his Commanding Officer was Group Captain Cyril Kay, a fine airman, who made the first through flight from London to Auckland in 1934. He was also a quiet chap and Johnny suspected that peacetime service would bring many quiet chaps to the fore; the boisterous days at Kenley, Biggin Hill and Horne were over. On his first day at Wigram, 3 December 1945, he met a ghost from the past, Squadron Leader Harry Lett, whom he had encountered as an unsympathetic flight commander at Taieri in 1940. 'I well remembered him for being so tough on me when I was trying my hardest to learn to fly, particularly in view of the fact that I had five instructors in nine hours flying.' Meeting again after four years, however, they got on much better. Johnny now realised more clearly the pressure under which Harry was working in those hectic days and Harry, for his part, was proud of his former pupil's splended wartime achievements.

Taieri came under Wigram's control at that time, making plenty of work for Johnny, who also found much discontent among men wishing to be released more rapidly than the service could allow. Fortunately, he enjoyed these new challenges, especially once he realised that Cyril Kay intended to let him deal with them in his own way. Whenever he could, he escaped from his desk into a cockpit. Few aircraft were available, but he flew them all (except the Dakotas) whenever he got the chance: Corsairs, Harvards, Oxfords and Tiger Moths.

More exciting than these, however, was another opportunity to fly a Gloster Meteor, one of the first generation jet fighters. This machine (a Mark III) had been presented to the Royal New Zealand Air Force by the Royal Air Force and after displays over various North Island towns arrived at Wigram for a South Island tour. To his great delight, Johnny was permitted to fly this beautiful aircraft from Taieri over Invercargill, his home town, on 6 May 1946. His delight was shared by his fellow-citizens, as the Town Clerk informed him on the 8th: 'I am directed by the Council to express to you their congratulations on your magnificent skill displayed during this exhibition under adverse weather conditions.' The day had been wet and windy, Johnny remembered, and the ventilator in the aircraft's nose jammed open: 'In the cockpit it felt just as if someone was spraying me with a fine garden hose.' Public interest was so great that business in the city was practically at a standstill until the demonstration was over. 'Hardly any traffic moved in the streets,' reported the *Southland Times*, 'and the roof tops of business buildings were crowded with spectators, despite the rain.' The occasion was even commemorated in verse in the same newspaper by F.W.G. Miller, a well-known Southland poet. It begins:

Oh yes I saw the Meteor
But still I have a grouse
To keep it in my sight I had
To scamper round the house,
And round and round and round I went
And nearly met disaster,
For with a roar the Meteor
Circled round much faster.

Cyril Kay was posted to England and for a few months Johnny served as station commander until Group Captain Frank Dix arrived. He then suffered a swift decline, losing not only his command but also his long-held rank of wing commander, even though he was at that time an honorary aide-de-camp to the Governor General, Sir Bernard Freyberg. Nothing was done to soften these blows. A peremptory telephone call from Wellington simply informed him that he was now a squadron leader. At the end of September 1946 he was officially assessed as an 'exceptional' pilot, an assessment that sadly amused him for he had flown just forty-nine hours in the last ten months; the hectic pace of wartime operations was indeed a fading memory. His private life, happily, provided ample compensation. Natalie and he were still enjoying the novelty of being together every day after years of separation and he was on the best of terms with a wide circle of friends and relations, old and new. Johnny acquired a delapidated Vauxhall Coupé (1936) upon which he lavished much loving care, restoring the engine and chassis and re-upholstering the interior. He also found like-minded spirits (not including Natalie, in this instance) with whom he could spend happy hours at Lake Ellesmere, soaked and frozen, shooting ducks.

In February 1947 Johnny recovered the acting rank of wing commander and in the following month was sent to Ohakea to undergo a conversion course on the Mosquito. He was probably more familiar with it than his instructors, having flown that aircraft frequently at the Empire Central Flying School in 1945. Nevertheless, he welcomed the opportunity to 're-convert' himself and give his whole attention to flying again, 'especially in such a lovely aeroplane'. Once officially converted, he went with three flight lieutenants to Auckland: Mick Walker (another pilot) and two navigators. From there, they flew in a TEAL Short Solent flying boat to Sydney on 20 March and travelled on by train to Amberley (near Brisbane) where four dual-control Mosquitos, purchased from the Royal Australian Air Force, awaited them. They were to fly two back to New Zealand and then return to Amberley to collect the other two. Not surprisingly, Johnny enjoyed almost every minute of these two unusual trips.

The Solent flight, his first experience of civilian standards of passenger comfort (though spoiling him for subsequent cold flights on hard seats in military transports) put him in the right mood for another first experience, that of Sydney. He and his three companions spent two exciting days there, discovering King's Cross (which shocked him more than wartime central London), before climbing aboard a train for Brisbane. That journey, lasting twenty-five endless hours, proved more of a nightmare even than rail travel in New Zealand. They did what they could to anaesthetise themselves with Australian-made liquor, but remained only too conscious of the flies, the heat and the noise as they clattered and lurched along, apparently on square wheels. Trundling through one wasteland, they saw men standing by the track, calling on passengers to throw out their newspapers; more orthodox deliveries, they were told, took a week. All things pass, however. They reached Brisbane at last and were driven out to Amberley where two Mosquitos were made ready for flight and ferried home safely via Sydney on 8 April.

A month later, Johnny returned to Sydney (in a Short Sandringham) with three officers, but this time they flew on (in an even more comfortable Skymaster) to an air training base at Point Cook, Melbourne. There they managed to arrange themselves a most pleasant week, diligently improving inter-service relations and broadening their social horizons, before flying via Canberra to Brisbane in a Dakota which, if less attractive than either the Sandringham or the Skymaster, still represented a distinct improvement on the train. But it took a fortnight to get the two Mosquitos remaining at Amberley into serviceable condition and they were then flown to Bankstown (Sydney) on 2 June, where bad weather and compass trouble kept them grounded for a further week. The trouble can be accepted as genuine (no mere ruse to prolong enjoyment of Sydney's delights) because the four New Zealanders had only two pounds between them. The RNZAF Liaison Officer refused to advance them money against their pay and though their accommodation and breakfast were free, other meals were not, and therefore Johnny saw plenty of the parks, museums, streets and harbour views of that great city on the strength of a pie and one glass of beer: 'It was really very good for us,' he reflected, 'because in fact, we saw a lot more of Sydney than we would have done if we'd had any money.' During these days, he learned that he had been appointed to a permanent commission and so his future seemed assured.

Johnny decided to make an attempt on the record for a crossing of the Tasman Sea, 'having every confidence,' he wrote later, 'in the wonderful Merlin engines behind which I had flown for so long.' He took off on the morning of 10 June 1947 (with Flight Lieutenant Kitson as his navigator) and climbed to 27,000 feet, the Mosquito's best cruising altitude. Two-thirds of the way home, he ran into a front and because the aircraft was icing up inside the cockpit as well as on the wings, he climbed to higher altitude and finally broke clear at 32,000 feet, but he now knew that his chance of breaking the record by a substantial margin was gone. He became more concerned about not breaking himself and his navigator 'because if the front lay over New Zealand, I could quite easily plough into the mountains'. Deciding to descend while still certain that he was over the sea, he circled round and down, taking ten minutes to get an altimeter reading of 300 feet, but even from that height the sea remained invisible. Levelling out on a northerly course, he let down further, very slowly, and soon struck heavy rain. His airspeed indicator began to work again (having frozen earlier) and finally he saw wave tops about 100 feet below. Turning back on course, he made a landfall at D'Urville Island, three hours thirty-eight minutes out from Bankstown. Twenty-two minutes later, he was over Ohakea. 'I did get the record,' he wrote, 'but it could have been a lot better.' The second Mosquito (flown by Mick Walker) arrived an hour later after a bad trip, flying most of the way in thick cloud at low altitude.

These visits to Ohakea and Australia provided a welcome change from Wigram, where he felt increasingly unhappy. Never a man to burden others with his troubles, he maintained his usual cheerful front at home and it was years before Natalie learned how he really felt at that time. Aeroplanes were being put in store, no systematic training — in the air or on the ground — was in progress, familiar faces disappeared and those that remained grew surlier; morale was the poorest he ever encountered, in or out of the service, and at one time the general discontent became positively mutinous.

Quite apart from the persistent grumbling of those who wanted their release from the service, Johnny was becoming aware of an unpleasant tension between the so-called 'Europeans' (officers and men who spent the war in Britain, France or the Mediterranean) and the 'Pacifics' (those who served at home or in the islands). The Europeans were held to be British-orientated, looking to the Royal Air Force for ideas and equipment, whereas the Pacifics were supposedly American-minded, preferring the ideas and equipment of the United States Air Force. In Johnny's opinion, the Air Department in Wellington showed neither energy nor imagination in explaining to the rank and file its policy regarding employment in the Royal New Zealand Air Force and as for the European-Pacific tension, alternative points of view which had much to commend them were not openly debated; they were allowed to degenerate into personal rivalries. Moreover, there were in the higher ranks officers who attempted — in some cases with enthusiastic support from their wives — to impose social customs regulating off-duty conduct that were more rigid and exclusive than those prevailing in the Royal Air Force. Both Johnny and Natalie found them inappropriate as well as distasteful. The New Zealand Air Force, they felt, should develop its own customs — customs that were more in keeping with New Zealand's more informal ethos. Neither saw any reason to be more British than the British.

Johnny left Wigram at the end of October 1947 and went to command the RNZAF Base in Fiji and No. 5 (Flying Boat) Squadron on 1 November as a substantive (paid) wing commander. Soon afterwards, Natalie was able to join him (until then, wives had not been permitted to accompany husbands overseas) and their first child was now on the way — Christopher John, who would be born on 1 April 1948. In Fiji, Johnny had some 300 officers and men under his command, supported by a large staff of Fijians and Indians, twenty 'marine hulls' (among them a high-speed launch, seaplane control launches, dinghies, cutters and bomb barges) and, best of all, three Catalina flying boats at Laucala

Bay. He immediately seized this heaven-sent opportunity to get into the air again in a famous aircraft that he had never flown before. Johnny loved Fiji. He was healthier, more alert and certainly better tempered now that he was immersed once again in the purposeful life of an active squadron. The fact that it was based in a group of attractive islands blessed with a beautiful climate was merely a bonus; he would have been almost as happy if it had been based in Antarctica.

The Checketts rented a house overlooking Suva Harbour and quickly made friends among the local people. They often dined with the Governor (Sir Brian Freeston) and Natalie was soon on genuinely friendly terms with Lady Freeston, especially after her son was born. Social life in Fiji was extremely active and the Checketts were on everyone's visiting list, partly because of Johnny's excellent war record and official position, partly because Natalie was an attractive young woman with a most pleasant manner. Johnny yielded to no man in his capacity to enjoy good company until a late hour, but he was glad to have Natalie to help him through the many formal occasions when colonial officials, visiting dignitaries and Fijian authorities (civil and military) were entertaining or being entertained.

Although Johnny loved the air, he also loved the sea and recognised that this posting gave him a wonderful — probably unrepeatable — chance to enjoy both to the utmost. He therefore resolved to have a little yacht built and so realise a boyhood dream. Some twenty-five years earlier, while visiting a whaling station in Stewart Island run by Norwegians, he had been given a detailed drawing of one of their neat little Pram dinghies. He salvaged some kauri planks from a wrecked barge, laid off one of the marine hands employed by the Royal New Zealand Air Force and paid him four pounds a week to build a vessel which he named *Pandora*. Timbers from that barge helped to build several more vessels and Johnny had them rigged with sails cut from old bedsheets. He formed a yacht club and organised regular regattas. He also joined the Suva Yacht Club and became the first winner of the Governor's Cup, presented to the club by Sir Brian Freeston. An open handicap race, it attracted a huge entry and a beautiful miniature of the actual cup remains one of Johnny's proudest possessions.

Even though service morale in Fiji was better than at Wigram,

Johnny sought to improve it in several ways. He insisted, for example, that all officers and men take an active part in a sport of their own choosing, believing that sport encouraged team spirit as well as physical fitness. He designed a smart mess kit (white jacket, blue trousers; still in use) for officers to wear on formal occasions. He arranged with a film company to supply films (stipulating that they must be recent and in good condition) and revived regular screenings in an open air cinema. He also made it his personal business to get to know everyone under his command, explaining the orders received from Wellington in straightforward language, listening to opinions and, in general, finding out for himself what was really going on. Nor did he mind lending a hand himself. One day, watching an airman making hard work of welding a cylinder, he asked if he could have a go — and did the job quickly and neatly.

Those islands were then very isolated. Apart from infrequent air links, severely limited in carrying capacity, only one ship a month connected them with New Zealand. Johnny therefore set himself to do everything he could to generate a happy family atmosphere among servicemen of all ranks, their wives and children; and to foster good relations with the Fijians. According to Tom Tweed (his Senior YMCA Officer), he enjoyed an outstanding success in these tasks, earning widespread respect and affection among those who knew him — service or civilian, at work or at play. In particular, Tom recalls his support for the appointment of a squadron chaplain, the encouragement he gave to scouting and his readiness to help the Roman Catholic sisters running a leper colony on Makogai Island.

When it became known that a certain AC2 Berryman had been posted to the marine section at Laucala Bay from Hobsonville, the news was greeted by high and low in that section with what seemed to Johnny ludicrous consternation. Berryman, apparently, had a reputation for spectacular acts of indiscipline. Calling to mind some of the pilots and ground crew whom he had seen off the leash in England, he doubted whether Berryman could match their capacity to frighten and destroy. He interviewed him on arrival, as he did all newcomers, and was surprised to find him a positively model airman, quiet and respectful.

That night, however, Berryman got roaring drunk, stole the station warrant officer's jeep, burst through the guard gate and ploughed half way across a paddy field before the engine gave up; six airmen, sent to pursue and subdue, were given a brisk workout before they got him down and still. He was brought before Johnny and asked for an explanation. 'Well, Sir,' he said, 'I was on the Skagerrak run from Sweden through to England with high-speed launches carrying ball-bearings and we got intercepted a few times by German surface craft and shot up. I was badly burned one night and sometimes, as a result of the hard war I had, I can't remember what I've done, particularly if I've a few beers in.' Unimpressed by this tale, even though he rightly believed it to be perfectly true, Johnny pulled open a drawer, took out his medals and laid them on the desk in front of him. 'Well, Berryman,' he said, 'I also had a bloody hard war and these prove it. So did lots of fellows who were never given medals. We like a drink too and take it without causing all this nonsense. How do you plead?' 'Sir,' he replied, 'I'm guilty as buggery.'

Even though Berryman's list of convictions covered four pages, Johnny decided not to add to it. He 'admonished' him (this being the lightest punishment possible and one not formally recorded), much to the ill-concealed displeasure of the station warrant officer and the adjutant. After Berryman was marched out of his office, Johnny told the adjutant: 'I want no victimisation of that bloke. You get the office girl to make two cups of tea and when they're ready, bring him back in here.' And so, over tea, he had his third meeting with Berryman in two days. This, he said, was the one break he would get; next time, it would be back to Auckland and a civil prison. But there would be no next time. Berryman soon showed himself a first class boatman and Johnny gave him control of a high-speed launch (acquired from the United States Navy, occasionally borrowed by the Governor) which he transformed into a thing of beauty, glossily painted and beautifully fitted out. 'Poor Berryman,' Johnny recalled. 'He was killed in a motorcycle accident in Auckland shortly after he left Fiji.'

Thomas McKinney, principal of the Ratu Kadavulevu School (about eighty kilometres from Suva) is one man who well remembers Johnny's time in Fiji. Thomas's infant son suddenly became very ill and needed more expert medical assistance than was then available in Fiji. He asked Johnny if he could help. The only serviceable Catalina had left for New Zealand that morning, but Johnny rang his friend Harold Gatty, a director of Pan American Airways, and arranged an immediate passage to Auckland for Thomas's wife and the child. He also arranged an RNZAF flight from Suva hospital to Nadi to catch the American aircraft. 'There is no doubt,' wrote Thomas McKinney in October 1985, 'that but for the help and influence of Wing Commander Checketts the child would have died within a day or two. As it was, he returned to Fiji three months later in excellent condition.' Thomas met Johnny in 1962 and reminded him of this dramatic incident, but 'he did not consider his action anything more than a good turn, hardly worth a mention, as he did not even enter it in his log'.

The Fijian Islands were swept by a fierce hurricane in December 1948 and Johnny was called on to carry out a survey of the damage done there and in the nearby Lau Group. Many houses and crops were destroyed and for some weeks his Catalinas were as busy as in wartime, transporting food and medical supplies to distant islands (often landing in uncharted waters), reporting on local conditions and estimating what further measures of immediate relief were needed. 'I had never seen so many trees torn down,' wrote one doctor, 'since I saw the terrible effects of shell fire and high explosive bombs in the European War.' After the crisis was over, Sir Brian Freeston showed himself warmly appreciative of the 'magnificent effort made by the RNZAF Detachment under your command. The keenness and efficiency of the Force have enabled us not only to ascertain accurately the extent of the hurricane damage through the Lau Islands, but also to send immediate relief where it was most badly needed. This has all been accomplished within a few days; without your assistance it would have taken several weeks. You have placed under a lasting debt of gratitude not only the people in the stricken Islands, but everyone else who has any responsibility for, or interest in, their welfare . . .'

When Johnny left Fiji in September 1949, the *Fiji Times and Herald* recorded that he would certainly be missed. 'He has not only been a most efficient commanding officer, but he has always been ready to help the Colony in every possible way. His co-operation immediately after the December hurricane in organising relief for the Lauans, who were so badly hit, and placing

Catalinas at the disposal of the Government to take food and medicines to distant islands will be long remembered. Undoubtedly his prompt action saved much suffering and probably many lives. He will carry with him the best wishes of the Fijian people.'

On returning to New Zealand in September, Johnny learned that he was to leave again at the end of October for even more distant parts: the Royal Air Force Staff College at Bracknell in Berkshire. The rapid translation from the tropics to an English winter was a sore trial to the Checketts' son Christopher (eighteen months old on 1 October), but his parents were thrilled to have this opportunity to visit people and places once so important to them both — to Johnny who lived among them and to Natalie who knew them only through his letters and the newspaper cuttings she had collected so diligently. They stayed at first in Oxted with the Ferguson family, dear friends to Johnny during the war, and resumed their friendship with Alan Deere and his wife Joan. Alan was then stationed near Oxted at Kenley, where Johnny had begun his career as a fighter pilot only eight years earlier, though it seemed at times more like eighty. Alan and Johnny had met briefly in New Zealand in February 1948, when Alan paid his first visit home for eleven years, and found that their friendship remained as warm as ever.

The Checketts saw in the New Year of 1950 at Biggin Hill and then departed for Bracknell in the middle of a bitterly cold winter. The course lasted the whole year and Wednesday afternoons brought the best part as far as Johnny was concerned, because he could then fly the college's Spitfire, weather permitting. As always, he made friends easily and enjoyed whatever leisure activities were either organised or permitted. Otherwise, he found the year extremely difficult. The exercises were realistic and interesting, but he continually felt the need of more time to complete them properly. Consequently, he burned a great deal of midnight oil. The pressure of work was deliberately varied, periods that were scarcely tolerable contrasted with periods of near idleness. This, he was told, simulated the actual pattern of staff work in wartime. Although he saw merit in this approach, he remembered staff officers who regarded working through the night as a good thing in itself, rather than an unavoidable response to a crisis; an action to impress top brass rather than to confound the enemy.

The best staff officers, he thought, like the best pilots and ground crews, got every essential job done without seeming unduly worried or even busy; they took a positive pride in not flapping, whatever the circumstances. But he kept quiet, deciding — perhaps wrongly — that such truths were best left undiscussed even at staff colleges.

Having escaped with a safe pass from Bracknell, Johnny joyfully seized the opportunity to do some serious and exciting flying, mainly at North Weald, where Herb Patterson (one of his old 485 Squadron pilots) served as adjutant to 601 (County of London) Squadron, Royal Auxiliary Air Force. He flew some ten hours during January 1951 in the Vampire V jet fighter, to familiarise himself with an aircraft then being bought by the Royal New Zealand Air Force. In February he was attached to 2 Group Headquarters, British Air Forces of Occupation in Germany, and visited many cities and aerodromes. The massive destruction wrought by aerial bombing (and ground fighting) was still evident everywhere, especially in Hamburg, where mounds of rubble had not yet been cleared away and the harbour was still littered with wrecked vessels of all shapes and sizes. The atmosphere, not surprisingly, was tense and unfriendly and a curfew, beginning at 9.30 p.m. each night, was strictly enforced. The general bleakness, exacerbated by bitterly cold weather, as well as the surliness of the Germans, horrifying stories of life and death in concentration camps and rumours of Russian aggression all combined to make this one of the most chilling experiences in Johnny's career. He was immensely relieved to return to England. Sadly, neither time nor funds permitted a visit to Johnny's friends in France before they sailed home to New Zealand in April 1951.

Johnny was sent to Ohakea in May to command the flying wing there, a posting which surprised him: at the end of the war, having-been awarded a Distinguished Pass at the Empire Central Flying School, he was given an administrative job; now, having been expensively trained in staff work, he was given a flying job. Not that he complained: the chance to fly regularly at Ohakea was infinitely preferable to the chore of paper-pushing in Wellington, the fate for which he had been steeling himself. The Vampires had not yet arrived and many of 75 Squadron's Mosquitos had a poor serviceability record. Johnny therefore grounded them all for a thorough overhaul, encouraged the hangar staffs to make a special effort, and soon had the whole squadron airborne again. He arranged several long-range navigation exercises, improving skill and morale alike, and (better still) a dredge was made available for target practice some fifty kilometres west of Westport, and smartly sunk.

The Vampires, arriving in August, were assembled at Hobsonville and test-flown by a de Havilland pilot out of Whenuapai. On 28 August, when they were ready for service use by the newly-formed 14 Squadron, Johnny had the privilege of flying the first of these excellent machines from Whenuapai to Ohakea. In February 1952 he gave a brilliant aerobatic display at New Plymouth when three Vampires were publicly demonstrated in New Zealand for the first time, a display which he repeated (with embellishments) in September before the Prime Minister, Mr Sidney Holland, and many of the country's senior civilian and military leaders. The occasion was a celebration at Ohakea to mark 14 Squadron's departure for Cyprus, 'the strategic nerve centre of the present world', in Mr Holland's opinion. Twelve Vampires gave a demonstration of formation flying and Johnny, who is not superstitious, performed in a thirteenth. Somewhat sadly, he bade farewell to the eager young pilots setting off on their great adventure. A few weeks later, he left Ohakea. In some respects, these had been the best days of his service in New Zealand. During this happy time in his career, the Checketts' second child — Mary-Jane Margaret — was born and named after both her grandmothers. Like her brother, she is an 'April Fool', born on 1 April, an odd coincidence that has long caused the whole family wry amusement.

In December 1952 Johnny was sent to command Taieri, the base where he learned to fly some twelve years earlier and would now be responsible for training a new generation. Though sorry to leave Ohakea, he recognised that he had enjoyed eighteen months there and while a training base must lack the excitement of an operational base, it was at least a *flying* base; he had once again avoided burial in a Wellington office. He therefore returned to his many friends and relations in the Deep South in good spirits, little realising that his service career would end at Taieri.

Young men summoned for compulsory military training were taught to fly the Tiger Moth there and then posted to the Reserve.

Some accepted both service and flying discipline willingly enough, others did not. Johnny had expected no less and this problem caused him no undue concern. What he had not anticipated, however, was persistent trouble with some of his instructors. Most of them were former wartime pilots and (in the right mood) perfectly capable airmen. But Johnny, by no means either a martinet or a wowser, found some of them ill-disciplined and too fond of drink for his taste. Constant agitation on this front was offset in part by the excellent co-operation he received from other instructors, especially from Pilot Officer David Crooks, who became a firm friend and, ultimately, Chief of Air Staff. Moreover, he was soon joined by an old 485 Squadron comrade, Ken Lee, as Engineering Officer and made another firm friend in Ken Moir, his Education Officer.

No. 4 Territorial Squadron was based at Taieri, equipped with Mustang fighters. Johnny thought these aircraft too high-powered for week-end pilots, out of regular practice, who were also sometimes careless, but Wellington ruled otherwise. Although one Mustang was written-off as a result of bad handling, for some time nothing worse occurred. Nevertheless, he had an uneasy feeling that there might be a serious accident one day and that he would be involved. This premonition of disaster proved, unfortunately, well-founded. Meanwhile, although Johnny sometimes flew these Mustangs himself, he contented himself more often with the squadron's Harvards. Whenever he flew the Harvard, he usually invited a deserving airman along for the ride. Gradually, as problems on the ground eased, he began to enjoy life at Taieri. Lewis Baker, brother of Reg (who played such a vital part in saving his life in May 1942 when he was shot down into the Channel), became a special friend and with other friends they often went fishing or duck shooting together.

A British submarine, the *Tactician*, arrived in Dunedin in September 1953 and Johnny became friendly with its commanding officer, Lieutenant-Commander H. R. Clutterbuck. Football matches were arranged between airmen and submariners, there were aeroplane joyrides, some jovial dinner parties and, not least, one or two serious drinking bouts all comfortably won by the submariners. Clutterbuck invited Johnny to travel in the submarine from Dunedin to Bluff and he gladly accepted, not daring to seek Wellington's prior permission. They left Dunedin in moonlight, travelling on the surface in a calm sea, and Johnny spent hours in the conning tower, gradually becoming frozen stiff but determined nevertheless to savour every moment of a unique journey. Regretting only that he had no opportunity to experience a crash dive or to travel submerged, he went ashore at Bluff and rushed to catch a train to Invercargill, where one of his pilots had been asked to pick him up in a Harvard and take him home to Taieri.

For the second time since the end of the war, Johnny was appointed to serve as aide-de-camp to the Governor General (now Sir Willoughby Norrie), and in this capacity was summoned to Auckland on 22 December 1953 to attend His Excellency on the occasion of the Queen's visit. The Tangiwai rail disaster occurred on Christmas Eve, greatly distressing everyone in New Zealand, not least the Queen and the Duke of Edinburgh. Already a confirmed monarchist, he found that these duties — in Auckland and later in Wellington — increased his admiration for the Queen and the Duke. In his opinion, they saw some of his fellow countrymen at their worst. Whenever they appeared in public, men and women would scramble frantically to get within range of them and then stare rudely, giving tongue to personal comments that could be clearly heard. As for those who managed to get themselves presented, some spoke in such an unctuous manner that the Royal couple must have been nauseated — unless, inwardly, they were shaking with laughter. In short, Johnny cringed throughout these occasions, longing for them to end. And yet, as far as he could see, neither the Queen nor her husband ever failed to smile pleasantly and speak courteously (in normal voices) whatever fawning twaddle was addressed to them. Having himself enjoyed the privilege of presentation to King George VI and other members of the Royal Family (among them the Queen while still a princess) on several occasions during the war, Johnny was immensely impressed by their graciousness and especially by their ability to find something personal to say to whomever they met.

Back at Taieri, the occasion of an Open Day gave Johnny a rare chance to undertake some demanding flying. He and Squadron Leader Max Hope put on a display of aerobatics in two Vampires that caused Ron Bush, a very experienced pilot and then instructor with the Otago Aero Club to say to his friend George Watson: 'You will never see better precision flying anywhere in the world.' George has never forgotten 'that thrilling display by Checketts and Hope'; the last, as it happened, of Johnny's distinguished career. On the evening of 16 September 1954, a pilot of No. 4 Territorial Squadron took up an airman passenger with him in a Harvard to practise night flying. The aircraft crashed into Hope Hill and both men were killed. A disaster long feared by Johnny had come at last, though he did not immediately realise how closely he himself would be involved. That squadron practised night flying once a month and on those nights, Johnny made it a rule to be present in the hangar, impressing the need for care and attention upon all concerned. But on the night of the accident, he was not in the hangar because he and Natalie were entertaining a newly-appointed administrative officer and his wife. It was the first time he had not attended night-flying. Had he been there, the pilot would not have broken standing orders against carrying a passenger at night and would have been specifically warned against one possible cause of the accident, aerobatic practice. He would have been permitted to fly, however, as many territorial pilots before him. It was only after the accident that Johnny learned that such pilots were not permitted to fly at night. The prohibition was contained in a file closed before he arrived at Taieri and, consequently, never seen by him. In fact, he had it dug out of the records and submitted to the Court of Inquiry. The Chief of Air Staff (Air Vice-Marshal Walter Merton) nevertheless held Johnny responsible for the accident. He was shattered by this decision, which he believed unjust, and submitted his resignation. It was accepted and he then received his first and only posting to Wellington: for three unhappy months he did all that there was to do (which was precisely nothing) in an office at Shelly Bay before being allowed to leave the service in March 1955. Although the consequences of the Hope Hill accident were largely responsible for Johnny's decision to resign, two other factors contributed. One was Natalie's uncertain health and worry about the effect of frequent changes of location and schools on their children's education, the other was his belief that aerial topdressing offered excellent prospects.

He was then just forty-three, an awkward age at which to take up a new career, and his feelings of bitterness towards the Royal New Zealand Air Force lasted for years. They were scarcely eased even by the letters and expressions of sympathy which came his way at this time. Aubrey Breckon (one of New Zealand's most famous bomber pilots) wrote to him from Woodbourne in February to say that he was 'terribly sorry' to hear that Johnny was leaving the service. 'The RNZAF should not let you go. You should be promoted forthwith and given a good job. You have a brilliant war record, experience and background and our small service can ill afford to lose such good types as yourself.' Ivan Mitchell, Joint Services Liaison Officer in Melbourne, wrote in similar vein: 'There will be many like myself who will sincerely regret your decision and the RNZAF have I am sure lost one of their finest leaders.'

CHAPTER THIRTEEN

# Dreaming of Flying: March 1955 to December 1985

On several occasions since his return to Taieri in December 1952, the Mayor of Dunedin (Leonard Wright) had spoken to Johnny about aerial topdressing, a technique not widely practised in New Zealand at that time. Leonard thought Johnny would be well advised to leave the Air Force and master that technique because he foresaw that aerial topdressing would become a very profitable business. Although Johnny listened politely and agreed that Leonard's advice might well be sound, he made it clear to him that he had no intention of seeking a new career.

The Hope Hill accident and its consequences changed his mind and he therefore formed a company in Dunedin with Leonard and a former All Black captain, Jack Manchester, to carry out aerial topdressing in Otago and Southland. In March 1955 he bought a Tiger Moth in poor condition from a pilot in Hastings and had it overhauled by the Otago Aero Club. Russell Coulter, formerly an instructor at Taieri and, like Johnny, recently resigned from the service, was engaged as principal pilot. Meanwhile, Johnny travelled widely in Otago and Southland, seeking orders from farmers and phosphate from manufacturers. These were difficult to get, but Johnny managed to arrange sufficient of both to justify at least one year's operation. On this basis, despite strong opposition from other topdressing companies, the Air Services Licencing Authority permitted him to go ahead.

Two jobs were safely completed and then, on 7 April, Russell crashed at Kuri Bush (near Dunedin) while carrying out the third job and though he was unhurt, the aircraft was destroyed. Johnny managed to get another Tiger Moth, but it was damaged by a car while parked at Taieri on the night of 10 May. Not surprisingly, Russell now lacked enthusiasm for the work and soon left the company. Johnny, who had supposed that his main task would be to obtain orders, found himself responsible for all the flying. Throughout that winter, he flew on practically every day the weather permitted, often from fields full of dangerous bumps and hollows. A true-bred Southlander, devoted to duck shooting and fishing, long spells of cold and damp did not trouble him and, as always, he loved every minute he could spend in the air, whatever the conditions. He would always land if he saw a cast ewe and pick her up. 'I felt sorry for the old girl,' he says. 'I suppose it was also because I saw myself as a farmer if things went well.'

The informality of life as a topdresser greatly appealed to him. For example, one farmer — Peter Vollweiler — recalls a time when Johnny had been invited to address the Milburn Young Farmers' Club, but failed to confirm the date. Peter was wondering how to contact him when he heard a Tiger Moth roar over his house. A stone was thrown out with a note wrapped round it, tied on by string: 'O.K. for meeting Monday night.' Thus did confirmation arrive, writes Peter, 'Checketts-style, delivered by Tiger Moth, neatly on our front lawn!' Another farming couple, George and Elsie McLeod of Brighton, Otago, recall him circling their home low enough to call out: 'Is the kettle boiling?' before landing in the nearest paddock. 'Warm-hearted, cheerful and kind,' they write, 'he had many friends.'

Johnny was reminded of wartime operations in that he had to fly whenever he could, stick close to the ground (keeping a sharp lookout for hills, trees and powerlines), identify and hit a particular target. He also experienced a similar satisfaction in carrying out a necessary task well and making new friends (among the farmers who employed him). In the services, however, pilots were not expected to arm their own aircraft and (apart from the absence of enemy aircraft and flak) Johnny found this obligation, which he shared with his loader-driver, Derek Shaw, the major difference in his new career. Phosphate was then sown from bags, which came to the farmer in lots of sixteen or twenty bags to the ton. Johnny had to help Derek and the farmer load these bags into a truck and then into his aircraft: 'It took about three minutes to sow five bags, which meant we didn't have much time between loads,' as Buff Scott, a Waikouaiti farmer, ruefully recalls. 'I often think of him when I see and hear a topdressing plane go by,' added Buff — twenty-seven years after Johnny's last landing.

In August 1955, Johnny bought a second Tiger Moth and a Land Rover converted to load phosphate into the aeroplane. Both machines needed plenty of attention, particularly the Land Rover, but Johnny was able to do the work himself. His home, which he saw little of in those busy days, was close to the Taieri aerodrome. It was from there that the Americans made their first flights to Antarctica, and Johnny would watch, fascinated, as their fully-loaded Dakotas took off with the help of JATO (Jet Assisted Take Off) bottles. He met some of the men who carried out these arduous and dangerous journeys, regretting that he could not fly with them. He regretted still more his departure from the Air Force, even though he enjoyed his new flying duties and was making money. His successor at Taieri, Wing Commander Paddy O'Brien, invited him to dine in the Mess — a gracious gesture which he greatly appreciated, for he missed service life very much. But time — and pride — rarely permitted him to take advantage of the invitation.

On a typical day, Johnny would take off from Taieri just after daybreak and collect Derek from his father's farm at Berwick. They would then fly to the place where they were sowing, Derek having taken the Land Rover there at the start of the job. In flat country, Johnny liked to sow very early in the morning, when there was usually little or no wind; in hilly country, however, a gentle breeze was desirable, to spread the phosphate widely. But sowing could not always wait upon ideal conditions and he soon earned a high reputation among farmers for accurate, thorough work. If Johnny could sow more than four tons an hour, he charged £3 5s a ton. In easy country — flat or rolling, with good access roads — these were his usual charges. But when he had to fly so far and so high over rugged country that he could not deliver four tons an hour, the farmer had to pay more: usually £18 an hour. Such farmers were therefore particularly anxious to get value for money and Johnny saw that they got it.

One engagement in November 1955 was at Greenvale, an attractive if rather shabby homestead in the Waikaia valley. By nightfall, there was still work to do, but next morning strong winds were blowing, preventing useful sowing. Johnny therefore decided to fly home and return on a calmer day. He had just got airborne, with Derek in the front hopper, and was turning downwind to port, when a sudden gust blew the aircraft on its back. Derek escaped with a shaking, but Johnny injured his back badly and the Tiger Moth was wrecked. Although Natalie urged him to abandon topdressing, he refused to give up a life which he found both enjoyable and profitable. As soon as he recovered from his injuries, he bought another Tiger Moth and engaged Ted Cuttance as loader-driver, Derek having decided to go shearing.

The family had moved to a former Presbyterian manse at Otokia, a large two-storeyed house near the Taieri River, with an old stable which Johnny swiftly converted into a workshop and store, full of bits of aircraft, trucks and topdressing equipment. The Checketts' now had a third child, a son named David, who was born blind and crippled in April 1956. He had to endure several lengthy operations and required a great deal of special care before he was able to see and walk. David's gradual restoration to normality was a wonderful consolation to Johnny and Natalie at a very difficult time in their lives.

Johnny and Ted Cuttance got on splendidly, business boomed and Johnny bought a second aircraft, employed a second pilot and then bought a Piper Super Cub which was much superior to the Tigers: faster, more comfortable and able to carry far more phosphate. Unfortunately, business suddenly fell off, the second pilot departed and Johnny had to work very hard to make a bare living. Then, on 14 September 1957, he nearly killed himself. While sowing over Ross Mitchell's farm at Heriot, Johnny noticed that the Piper's oil pressure was low. 'On the run-in to the paddock, I had to clear a line of macrocarpa trees,' he remembers. 'But I was concentrating on trying to get the oil gauge to function and when I looked up I was only about six metres away from the trees and they were above me. So I switched off the engine and ploughed into them.' George Anderson, living in a cottage near the trees, heard the engine stop and an instant later the shocking noise of metal and branches crashing together. Rushing to the side of his house, he saw the shattered aircraft fall into a paddock. When George dragged Johnny clear of the wreckage, he was unconscious and his clothing drenched in petrol. He came round in hospital, realised he was lucky to be alive and promised Natalie to give up the business as soon as he could. To meet existing orders, he chartered another Piper and hired a pilot — who promptly wrecked it. This was the last straw. He had to resume flying himself, more intensively than ever, to complete those orders, find new ones and build up a business worth selling. His energetic last fling enabled him to sell up at a fair price in July 1958. Natalie was relieved and delighted, especially when the proceeds proved sufficient to buy a house at East Taieri. Since then, he has piloted an aircraft only occasionally. He was last at the controls in March 1984, soon after his seventy-second birthday.

Johnny was employed as a salesman of agricultural chemicals and all manner of household hardware for four years by his former partner (then Mayor of Dunedin and now knighted as Sir Leonard Wright) until he was appointed Secretary-Manager of the Otago Acclimatisation Society in July 1963 from a field of eighty applicants. Early British settlers in New Zealand formed these societies to help 'acclimatise' animals, birds and fishes introduced from Britain. He held the job for nine years, administering the Wildlife and Fisheries Act in regard to game hunting, protection of native birds and the fishing of trout and salmon. Exploring the hills, forests and streams of country that he knew well from the air was work that he loved. One of his most enjoyable tasks was to help protect an albatross colony at Taiaroa Head on the northern tip of the Otago Peninsula; it is the only mainland colony in the world. But bickering between anglers and hunters gradually wore him down. When the North Canterbury Acclimatisation Society (based in Christchurch) advertised for a secretary he therefore decided to apply, partly to escape a tense atmosphere and partly to be near Natalie's widowed mother, who was in poor health. He got the job and the Checketts family moved north in 1973 to a house in Hudson Street — named "Biggin Hill", as was his East Taieri home — where he soon displayed a hitherto concealed gift for producing beautiful flowers. He also earned himself a framed citation from the Nature Conservation Council 'for being active on conservation issues and in particular bringing public awareness to the effects of water pollution'.

His cousin, Karl Scott, honoured him at this time when selling a block of land at Oaklands, Halswell (a Christchurch suburb) by arranging that one street be named 'Checketts Avenue'. Unfortunately, conflict between anglers and hunters proved even more bitter in North Canterbury than it had been in Otago. Worse still, Johnny came to disagree with the Society's ruling council about both his own powers of action and its policies on breeding and liberation. Although some of the many meetings which he was obliged to attend became too acrimonious for his taste, he stuck the job for five years before finding much more congenial part-time work with a firm making leather stamping tools until he formally retired in 1982 at the age of seventy.

Meanwhile, in August 1973, David Crooks was appointed Commanding Officer at Wigram. He had served under Johnny at Taieri in 1953 and knew that he had left the service prematurely in unhappy circumstances. On learning that Johnny now lived in Christchurch, David resolved to bring him back into the fold. Johnny was invited to the Mess and though at first he came reluctantly, he is too affectionate by nature to resist friendly gestures. David and his senior officers went out of their way to make him feel part of the service team again. In 1975 he was made an honorary member of the No. 1 Officers' Mess at Wigram. Such membership is granted sparingly, usually to civic dignitaries, and is not normally renewed year after year. But Johnny's was, until finally he was made the only honorary *life* member of the Mess in New Zealand. These marks of favour mean much to him, for he has greatly valued the opportunity to be in regular touch with the Royal New Zealand Air Force once more, meeting again pilots and ground crew with whom he had served over twenty years earlier. Soon after returning home from his visit to Biggin Hill in 1978, John Robertson, Secretary of Defence in Wellington, wrote to him. 'I am sure you realise,' he said, 'that a great many of your friends in the RNZAF and in the Ministry were keen that by hook or by crook you should get the opportunity to once again relive the memories of your wonderful service in the Second World War.' These generous words touched Johnny deeply.

The Royal New Zealand Air Force began a fund-raising campaign for its museum at Wigram in 1982 and Johnny willingly offered to help with the accounts. A few months later, Group Captain Colin Rudd (then C.O. at Wigram) discussed with Johnny the restoration of a Tiger Moth suitable for display out of a jumble of spare parts long stored in a hangar. Many were broken or rusted, others missing, and the project lapsed until January 1984 when Group Captain Ross Donaldson, Colin's successor, revived it in talks with Arch Beazer, formerly a pilot and later an engineer with vast experience both in civil and military aviation. Arch quickly gathered a team of assistants, of whom Johnny was one — glad to abandon the accounts in favour of more practical assistance to the museum. Invited to report one morning to Wigram, Arch Beazer and his men were issued with protective clothing: long white coats which ensured that they were known as 'the Moth Doctors'. More than a year later, their 'patient' was beautifully restored and in 1985 became a static exhibit in the Royal New Zealand Air Force Museum. Hours of regular work at a self-imposed task made the Moth Doctors great friends, justly proud of their achievement.

But their aircraft cannot fly and Ross Donaldson therefore asked Johnny if he knew of another moribund Tiger Moth that could be made airworthy. His brother-in-law, Rex Grover, put him in touch with George Kingsbury, a farmer at Rakaia (some fifty kilometres south of Christchurch) who had two such machines and offered to give one to the RNZAF if the other was restored to flying condition for his own use. And so the Moth Doctors are now treating two more patients. Quite apart from their friendship with each other, they enjoy the wholehearted co-operation of the senior officers at Wigram and the staffs of the Technical Wing and Carpenters' Shop. 'We have all the fun of being in the service,' says Johnny, 'without any of the drawbacks.' Much of the 'fun' is in fact hard work, for 'some of the wings were in a dreadful state, full of birds' nests and guff; there was also a lot of rust and corrosion. But we finally reduced both machines to a heap of nuts, bolts and spars and have begun to re-assemble them.'

The Tiger Moths were flying again by April 1987, when the museum was officially opened by the Governor General, Sir Paul Reeves, to mark the 50th anniversary of the founding of the RNZAF. John Barry was in charge, followed by David Provan, and then Therese Angelo who now has the responsibility. It was a project dear to Johnny's heart, 'ever since it was a mere thought', he used to say. Whatever grief or even bitterness he felt during his last days of active service at Taieri and Shelly Bay was well and truly forgotten.

After serving as a Moth Doctor, he spent some years as a guide at the museum, chatting easily with young and old about all the exhibits. The museum now has on display some 25 aircraft, among them a very rare Avro 626 and such uncommon types as a De Havilland Beaver, a Hawker Siddeley Andover, a Lockheed Hudson, a Bristol Freighter, a McDonnell Douglas Skyhawk and, of course, a Spitfire – a Mark XVI, somewhat later than the models in which Johnny made his name. He knew all their histories and particularly liked that of the Avenger. 'A monstrous great thing', he called it, 'I wouldn't dare land such a beast on an aircraft carrier bucking about at sea.' The Avenger, he told everyone, began life as a deadly torpedo bomber and then became a sad target tug, a sadder aerial topdresser and saddest of all a gate guardian before finding 'a happy resting place in our lovely museum.' Younger men took over from the Moth Doctors and are now rebuilding, when they can get the parts, an Airspeed Oxford, a Curtiss P-40 Kittyhawk and – rarer still – a Vickers Vildebeest. Apart from the displays, the museum includes ever-growing archives with numerous unpublished documents, logbooks and an impressive collection of rare as well as recent aviation books. On 1 April 2007 Wigram hosts an international conference to mark the RNZAF's 75th anniversary and Johnny will be there in spirit to remind everyone, in his modest, genial way, how much we all owe to New Zealand's airmen: past, present and to come.

# Afterword

Johnny Checketts was known to me long before I met him. His name and exploits were part of the air legend with which I grew up as a schoolboy in New Zealand during and after World War II. Our paths first crossed in December 1952 when we arrived at Taieri within days of each other in somewhat dissimilar circumstances: I was a Pilot Officer, fresh off wings course on posting to my first squadron; he was a Wing Commander, a much-decorated fighter ace taking over command of the station. My recollections of reporting in to the 'Old Man' are still clear: the sharp blue eys with a lurking twinkle, the warm vigorous handshake and the first words — 'Hello, son [it was always "son"], good to have you in the team. We're both new boys here, but you'll have the more fun. Off you go now and get into the air.' I had a date with a Mustang and needed no second bidding.

There followed memorable and happy days. In a territorial squadron full of wartime veterans a new boy quickly learned his place — at the bottom of the pecking order! But when we gathered in the Mess at the end of the flying day for the usual round, Johnny always made sure that the tyro was not left out. 'Come and join us, son,' he'd say, 'let's hear what you've been up to.' It was during these sessions that I began to see what kind of fighter leader he had been. In my time at Taieri, the Royal New Zealand Air Force was still coping with the problems of peacetime reconstruction. There was some feeling, which I only vaguely comprehended then, between the European and Pacific warriors. But I knew enough to have an increasing sympathy with and respect for the man wrestling with such problems.

Like many others of his generation, Johnny had been catapulted from a remote tranquillity to centre stage in earth-shaking events. The marks showed, but so did the qualities. The stern face of command could never quite conceal a natural warmth and charm;

175

boyish enthusiasm and sparks of a fiery competitive urge were never far beneath the surface. There was also a restlessness common in those adjusting from the high drama of wartime to the quiet routine of a more peaceful world. But, best of all, he had a natural dignity, personal rectitude and that intangible charismatic quality which marks out leaders.

Johnny had left the service when I returned to Taieri as adjutant of my original squadron. We met socially on a few occasions and I was struck by expressions of wistfulness as we chatted about old days. Although generally aware of the circumstances surrounding his departure, it was some years before I discovered the details. Characteristically, Johnny never mentioned them. Years later, while commanding at Wigram, I learned that he was now living in Christchurch. He had had practically no contact with his old service in nearly twenty years when we met again on the steps of the Officers' Mess. He had aged, but the blue eyes still shone warmly — and not without emotion — as we clasped hands. Since then, he has re-established a place with the Air Force he loves, giving freely of his time, talents and energy. A father figure now, he has identified with a new generation of youngsters to bring meaning to events which for them are ancient history. We often meet, and I am always moved by his enormous pride in the service and his continuing desire to make a contribution.

I was delighted to learn that Dr Vincent Orange had written Johnny's story. It is part of our general history as well as our service heritage — and representative of the many others whose stories will not be told. Yet it remains a personal record of one man's experience, set down with sympathy and understanding. What emerges is a very human tale in a dramatic setting. References to Johnny's early struggles during flying training, his initial self-consciousness on joining a squadron at war, his self-doubt before belated success in aerial combat, his worries and fears — all make for a vivid narrative. Johnny grows in stature as inherent grit and determination prevail and the responsibilities of leadership shift his focus of concern to others.

I count it a privilege to have been asked to write the final words of this book. I had the singular good fortune to meet Johnny Checketts early in my career and thus become the beneficiary of an association which grew to personal friendship. As a mark of my satisfaction in seeing him return to the fold, I shall conclude with the words of greeting I used on that occasion: 'Welcome home, Johnny!'

David M. Crooks, CB, OBE, RNZAF.

# Notes

CHAPTER ONE

Unless otherwise indicated, all material in this (and every) chapter is drawn from Wing Commander Checketts' personal papers and memories. See also H. L. Thompson, *New Zealanders with the Royal Air Force*, vol. ii, pp. 188-91 (a typical day at Biggin Hill); *Otago Daily Times*, 26 February 1972 (tankard); Bruce Scott, Christchurch *Star*, July 1977 (Checketts on air combat); Terry Gardiner, personal comment, 18 August 1985.

CHAPTER TWO

*Southland Times*, 26 January 1978 (Invercargill South School), 3 March 1920 (Dickson) and 10-13 March 1933 (Kingsford Smith); J. O. P. Watt, *Centenary of Invercargill Municipality, 1871-1971*, p. 57 ('flu epidemic); George Sutherland, personal comment, 24 November 1985; J. E. Johnson, *The Story of Air Fighting*, pp. 293-4 (fighter pilots).

CHAPTER THREE

W. G. G. Duncan Smith, *Spitfire into Battle*, pp. 10 (Tiger Moth) and 13-14 (Master); Bob Penniket (25 October 1985) and Jim Maxwell (22 October 1985), personal comments; *The Mouchotte Diaries*, p. 48 (Hurricane).

CHAPTER FOUR

Doug Brown's letters, on Wells and 485 Squadron; Kenneth G. Wynn, *A Clasp for 'The Few': New Zealanders with the Battle of Britain Clasp*, pp. 106-117 (on Deere) and 419-23 (on Wells); Alan C. Deere, *Nine Lives*, pp. 20 (origins), 201-2 (Checketts), 183-90 (escorts), 190 (Rhubarbs, deflection shooting) and 213 (Fw 190); Johnson, *op. cit.*, p. 111 (deflection shooting); *The Mouchotte Diaries*, p. 126 (ground crews); J. B. Priestley, *BBC Listener*, 17 May 1945 (1942); J. R. Smith and Antony Kay, *German Aircraft of the Second World War*, pp. 173-4 (Fw 190); stills from Robson's film of 4 April 1942 appear in Kevin W. Wells, *An Illustrated History of the New Zealand Spitfire Squadron*, p. 74, wrongly dated 4 May.

## CHAPTER FIVE

Laddie Lucas (ed.), *Wings of War,* p. 237 (Atcherley); Doug Stokes, *Paddy Finucane,* pp. 154-5; B. Collier, *The Defence of the United Kingdom,* pp. 292-4 and F. H. Hinsley (and others), *British Intelligence in the Second World War,* vol. ii, pp. 269-71 (claims and statistics); Doug Brown, personal comment, 22 October 85.

## CHAPTER SIX

Thompson, *op. cit.,* ii. 187 and 197 (Biggin Hill, Checketts and 485 Squadron); Colin Hodgkinson, *Best Foot Forward,* pp. 166 and 168-9 (Checketts and Biggin Hill); Priestley, *op. cit.* (British fellowship); AIR 50/173 (PRO, London), 611 Sqn. Combat Reports; Hinsley, *op. cit.,* ii. p. 520 (claims); Alfred Price, *World War II Fighter Conflict,* p. 158 (dogfight); Ken Branson, personal comment. October 1985; Deere, *op. cit.,* pp. 229-44 and *The Mouchotte Diaries,* pp. 186-94 (events and operations at Biggin Hill); W. J. A. Wood, 'Biggin Hill's Thousandth Kill' in *Royal Air Force Year Book, 1976,* pp. 59-64; Roger A. Freeman, *Mighty Eighth War Diary,* pp. 6 (claims), 38 (15 February), 50-51 (4-5 April) and 68 (22 June); Michael J. F. Bowyer, *2 Group RAF,* pp. 308-15 (75 Squadron Venturas); Wells, *op. cit.,* p. 165 (claims); Roland Winfield, *The Sky Belongs to Them* (autobiography); Alan Deere, personal comment, 12 April 1985; Doug Brown's letters, on Checketts.

## CHAPTER SEVEN

Marty Hume (10 March 1985), Doug Brown (22 October 1985), Leslie White (12 October 1985) and Ken Lee (October 1985) personal comments; Laddie Lucas, *Five Up,* pp. 86 and 91 (squadron leader and finger four); Duncan Smith, *op. cit.,* p. 112 (squadron leader); Johnnie Houlton, *Spitfire Strikes,* pp. 107 and 246 (finger four and claims of 9 August); AIR 50/159 (PRO, London), 485 Sqn. Combat Reports; Jim Haun, personal comment, 23 October 1985; Doug Brown's letters, on 27 July and Checketts' DFC; Thompson, *op. cit.,* ii. 191-3 (27 July and 9 August); Deere, *op. cit.,* 234-5 and 247-50 (Clostermann and Mouchotte); *The Mouchotte Diaries,* pp. 196 and 206-20 (last entry and death); Pierre Clostermann, *The Big Show,* pp. 45-50 (Mouchotte's death); Freeman, *op. cit.,* p. 76 (14 July and Pappy Walker); Christchurch *Press,* 13

August 1943 (9 August); AIR 168/4 (N.Z. National Archives) on Checketts in 1943; Errol Braithwaite, *Pilot on the Run* (on Leslie White's escape).

## CHAPTER EIGHT

AIR 50/159 (PRO, London), 485 Sqn., Final Intelligence Report; Deere on Checketts in Houlton, *op. cit.,* p. xii; Deere, *op. cit.,* pp. 251-2 and Thompson, *op. cit.,* ii. 196-7 (6 September); Doug Brown's letters, on Checketts as POW; Checketts' Statement re France, 28 October 1943 and information re Haddock from Air Historical Branch, London; account in *Evening Star,* Dunedin, 22 and 29 August 1964 and Laddie Lucas (ed.), *Wings of War,* pp. 261-2.

## CHAPTER NINE

Information re Kearins from Air Historical Branch, London, and from Edith Kearins, Mme Massé Solange and René Guittard; Airey Neave, *Saturday at M.I.9,* pp. 16-24 and 226-7; M. R. D. Foot and J. M. Langley, *MI9,* pp. 35, 55-63 and 207-212; J. M. Langley, *Fight Another Day,* pp. 242-3; Doug Brown's letters, 6 November 1943.

## CHAPTER TEN

Deere, *op. cit.,* p. 230 (Martell); AIR 26/206 (PRO, London), Ops. Record Book of 142 Wing; *The Mouchotte Diaries,* p. 159 (zigzagging); B. Collier, *op. cit.* p. 370 (V1 as Ford); Sir Trafford Leigh-Mallory, *Air Operations by the Allied Expeditionary Air Force in N.W. Europe from November 15th 1943 to September 30th, 1944,* para. 331 (130 and 303 Squadrons).

## CHAPTER ELEVEN

Christopher Hibbert, 'The Gamble at Arnhem', in *Purnell's History of the Second World War,* vol. v., no. 12, pp. 2108-2124; *The Studio,* vol. 135, no. 658 (January 1948), pp. 22-5 (appreciation of Dring); Desmond Scott, *Typhoon Pilot,* pp. 142-3 and Oliver Walker, *Sailor Malan,* pp. 89-90 (Checketts); Francis Chichester, *The Lonely Sea and the Sky,* p. 248 (nought feet navigation).

## CHAPTER TWELVE

*Southland Times,* 7 May 1946 (Meteor); Tom Tweed (26 November 1985), Thomas McKinney (12 October 1985) and George Watson (18 October 1985), personal comments.

## CHAPTER THIRTEEN

Janic Geelen, *The Topdressers,* pp. 252-3, 318, 324 and 329 (Checketts Aerial Topdressing Co., Ltd.); Peter Vollweiler (14 October 1985), E. N. (Buff) Scott (23 October 1985), George and Elsie McLeod (20 October 1985) and Ross Mitchell (17 February 1986), personal comments; *Otago Daily Times,* 16 November 1967 (Albatross Colony).

# Bibliography

*Unpublished Sources*

National Archives, Wellington: AIR 117/55 (press cuttings re Checketts), AIR 118/13 (Fighter Command in 1943), AIR 168/4 (Checketts in 1943), AIR 187/2 (Ohakea Ops. Record Book), AIR 191/3 (Taieri Ops. Record Book), AIR 204/2 (Laucala Bay Ops. Record Book). Public Record Office, London: AIR 50/173 (611 Sqn. Combat Records), AIR 50/159 (485 Sqn. Combat Records), AIR 26/206 (142 Wing Ops. Record Book).

Private communications: Ken Branson, Doug Brown, Alan Deere, Terry Gardiner, René Guittard, Jim Haun, Marty Hume, Edith Kearins, Ken Lee, Mme Massé Solange, Thomas McKinney, George and Elsie McLeod, Jim Maxwell, Ross Mitchell, Bob Penniket, E. N. (Buff) Scott, George Sutherland, Tom Tweed, Peter Vollweiler, Leslie White.

*Printed Sources*

Bowyer, Michael J. F., *2 Group RAF: A Complete History, 1936-1945* (Faber & Faber, London, 1974)

Brathwaite, Errol, *Pilot on the Run* (Hutchinson, New Zealand, 1986)

Chichester, Francis, *The Lonely Sea and the Sky* (Hodder & Stoughton, London, 1964)

Clostermann, Pierre, *The Big Show: Some Experiences of a French Fighter Pilot in the R.A.F.* (Chatto & Windus, London, 1951; Corgi paperback, 1965)

Collier, Basil, *The Defence of the United Kingdom* (H.M.S.O., London, 1957)

Deere, Alan C., *Nine Lives* (Hodder Paperbacks, London, 1959)

Dring, William, appreciation by P. D. Nairne in *The Studio*, vol. 135, no. 658 (January 1948) pp. 22-5

Duncan Smith, W. G. G., *Spitfire into Battle* (John Murray, London, 1981)

Foot, M. R. D. & J. M. Langley, *MI9: The British secret service that fostered escape and evasion 1939-1945 and its American counterpart* (Bodley Head, London, 1979)

Franks, Norman L. R., *Sky Tiger: The Story of Sailor Malan* (William Kimber, London, 1980)

Freeman, Roger A., *Mighty Eighth War Diary* (Jane's, London, 1981)

Geelen, Janic, *The Topdressers* (Aviation Press, Te Awamutu, 1983)

Hibbert, Christopher, 'The Gamble at Arnhem' in *Purnell's History of the Second World War*, vol. v., no. 12, pp. 2108-2124

Hinsley, F. H. (and others), *British Intelligence in the Second World War* (H.M.S.O., London, 3 vols., 1979, 1981 & 1984)

Hodgkinson, Colin, *Best Foot Forward* (Odhams, London, 1957; Corgi paperback, 1978)

Houlton, Johnnie, *Spitfire Strikes: A New Zealand Fighter Pilot's Story* (John Murray, London, 1985)

Johnson, J. E., *The Story of Air Fighting* (Hutchinson, London, 1985)

Kay, C. E., *The Restless Sky* (Harrap, London, 1964)

Langley, J. M., *Fight Another Day* (Collins, London, 1974; Methuen Paperbacks, 1980)

Leigh-Mallory, Sir Trafford, *Air Operations by the Allied Expeditionary Air Force in N.W. Europe from November 15th, 1943 to September 30th, 1944*, supplement to *The London Gazette*, 31 December 1946

Lucas, Laddie, *Five Up: A Chronicle of Five Lives* (Sidgwick & Jackson, London, 1978)

Lucas, Laddie, (ed.), *Wings of War: Airmen of All Nations Tell Their Stories, 1939-1945* (Hutchinson, London, 1983)

*The Mouchotte Diaries*, ed. André Dezarrois, trans. from French by Phillip John Stead (Staples Press, London, 1956)

Neave, Airey, *Saturday at M.I.9* (Hodder & Stoughton, London, 1969)

Price, Alfred, *World War II Fighter Conflict* (Macdonald & Jane's, London, 1975)

Priestley, J. B. 'Journey into Daylight' in *BBC Listener,* 17 May 1945

Scott, Desmond, *Typhoon Pilot* (Secker & Warburg, London, 1982)

Smith, J. R. & Antony Kay, *German Aircraft of the Second World War* (Putnam, London, 1972)

Sortehaug, Paul, 'A Year of Battle' in *Cassidy Group Bulletin,* vol. v., no. 2 (May 1971) p.5

Stokes, Doug, *Paddy Finucane: Fighter Ace* (William Kimber, London, 1983)

Thompson, H. L., *New Zealanders with the Royal Air Force* (War History Branch, Department of Internal Affairs, Wellington: 3 vols., 1953, 1956 & 1959)

Walker, Oliver, *Sailor Malan* (Cassell, London, 1953)

Watt, J. O. P., *Centenary of Invercargill Municipality, 1871-1971* (Times Printing Service, Invercargill, 1971)

Wells, Kevin W., *An Illustrated History of the New Zealand Spitfire Squadron* (Hutchinson of New Zealand, 1984)

Winfield, Roland, *The Sky Belongs to Them* (William Kimber, London, 1976)

Wood, W. J. A., 'Biggin Hill's Thousandth Kill' in *Royal Air Force Year Book, 1976* (RAF Benevolent Fund, London, 1976) pp. 59-64

Wynn, Kenneth G., *A Clasp for 'The Few': New Zealanders with the Battle of Britain Clasp* (Published by the Author, P.O. Box 1382, Auckland, 1981)

# Index